Robert Needham Cust

Essays on religious conceptions

Robert Needham Cust

Essays on religious conceptions

ISBN/EAN: 9783337261412

Printed in Europe, USA, Canada, Australia, Japan

Cover: Foto ©Lupo / pixelio.de

More available books at **www.hansebooks.com**

ESSAYS

ON

Religious Conceptions.

BY

ROBERT NEEDHAM CUST, LL.D.

Ἡ δὲ Σοφία πόθεν εὑρέθη;
Ποῖος δὲ τόπος ἐστὶ τῆς Ἐπιστήμης;
Εἶπε δὲ ἀνθρώπῳ·
Ἰδοὺ ἡ θεοσέβεια ἐστὶ Σοφία·
Τὸ δὲ ἀπέχεσθαι ἀπὸ κακῶν ἐστὶν Ἐπιστήμη.

SEPTUAGINT: *Job,* xxviii, 12, 28.

LONDON
LUZAC & CO., 46, GREAT RUSSELL STREET.

1898.

PREFACE.

These Essays have been written in a profound, and undoubting, Belief in the Dispensation of Christianity, as given to us in the pages of the New Testament.

The Belief is neither superficial, nor formal, nor conventional, but based on a lifelong study, not only of the New Testament, but of the Sacred Books of all other Religious Conceptions of Ancient days, and the Modern Religious Conceptions, which have sprung into existence in this century. In 1894, I published an Essay on the "Ancient Religious Conceptions of the World before the great Anno Domini," and in 1897 I published an Essay on the "Modern Religious Conceptions of the World," not in the usual style of prejudiced abuse, but a dispassionate and impartial description, as of a matter of Abstract Science, where Truth only is sought.

We are taught in Scripture that:

"God so loved the World" (*the whole World*), "that He gave His only begotten Son, that whosoever believeth in Him should not perish, but have everlasting Life."

And, again, in our prayers we repeat the words:

"Merciful God, who hast made all men, and hatest *nothing that Thou hast made*." (Book of Common Prayer: Collect for Good Friday.)

"We give Thee thanks for Thy goodness and lovingkindness to us, and *to all men*." (Book of Common Prayer: General Thanksgiving.)

How, then, can be justified the gross abuse in the Reports of Missionaries in the Field, of the poor non-Christian races, and their Beliefs, those poor races, who by the Divine Will never had, until this century, the knowledge of Divine Truth brought home to them by Apostle or Evangelist?

I entirely admit, that there were in the earlier Religious Conceptions faint anticipations, and foreshadowings, of some of the Doctrines of Christianity: the Trinity, God in Human Form suffering for his fellow-men, the presence of the Holy Spirit in the voice of Conscience, the Fatherhood of God openly expressed, the Immortality of the Soul, a Future State of Rewards and Punishments, and Faith in One Powerful to Save. In the fulness of time all these floating Conceptions, dimly seen in the non-Christian Sacred Books, the gift of God to the earlier races through Heaven-sent Messengers, became refined, expanded, and explained as part of the New and Final Conception, which came into existence in Judaea in the great Anno Domini.

I firmly believe in, and recognize, the presence of God in all the ages. In sundry times and divers manners, the Great Creator condescended to make Himself known to His poor children, lending them sparks of Divine Knowledge, here a little, there a little, till in the great Anno Domini was consolidated the one great Plan of Salvation; than which I submit, Human Wit never has devised anything more perfect and more sufficient for the wants of the Human race.

The pure Gospel of the New Testament, however, has been painfully deformed by the mediaeval admixture of Pagan and Hebrew survivals of the Elder Religious Conceptions, Anthropomorphism, Formality, Temple-Worship, and Ritual, and the elevation of some of God's faithful servants to the position of Demigods, having altars dedicated to them, and prayers uttered to them; and we are still blindly and vainly attempting to convey to great Oriental races, such as the inhabitants of India and China, the pure and simple Oriental Doctrines of Christ in a complicated European Occidental capsule, which those great races will surely decline to receive, until they are purged from mediaeval accretions and restored to their simple purity.

Those great Oriental races will be of opinion, that it has been a narrowing down of the Power, Wisdom, and Love of the Creator to hold, that by His decree all the possibilities of Worship, Divine Knowledge, and Spiritual Development, were for many centuries tied up and given, as a monopoly, to one miserable tiny race, such as the Hebrew, while Millions and Millions, black, white, red, yellow, and brown, were living, flourishing, feeling after God, if haply they could find Him, without any knowledge being imparted to them of the Great Truths conveyed to the Hebrew, though only to be treated by them with thankless scorn, and without their making the slightest effort during the centuries betwixt Moses, and the great Anno Domini, to convey them to adjacent tribes of their own Semitic Family, though they were quite ready themselves to adopt the vilest form of Worship of their neighbours (Ezekiel, viii, 9).

My object has been humbly
"To Justify the Ways of God to Man."

London, November, 1897.

CONTENTS.

PAGE

I.
THE DAWN OF A RELIGIOUS CONCEPTION 7

II.
THE DECAY OF A RELIGIOUS CONCEPTION . . . 23

III.
THE USELESS PROLONGATION OF THE LIFE OF A RELIGIOUS CONCEPTION BEYOND THE EPOCH, FOR WHICH IT WAS INTENDED 38

IV.
THE SUPERIOR EXCELLENCE OF A RELIGIOUS CONCEPTION, EVIDENCED BY THE RESULTS 75

(1) A calm, and fearless, and unsparing, comparison of its tenets with those of every other Conception, Past, Present, or dimly visioned in the Future, when purified from the degrading survivals of previous Religious Conceptions of the race.

(2) The unconquerable desire of those, who believe in it, to extend it to other races, and the whole of mankind by peaceful argument, unselfish sacrifice, and inducements wholly free from carnal advantages.

V.
THE PHILOSOPHICAL ASPECT OF THE IDEA OF METEMPSYCHOSIS 109

This Volume is dedicated by a Septuagenarian

to all those,

who care to examine scientifically, and study truthfully,

the story of the

Relation of the Human Soul to God

in all Ages, Regions, and degrees of Culture; and who humbly

rejoice in being

"Heirs of all the Past Ages,"

and being in possession of freedom of thought,

and accumulation of Knowledge,

which Holy Men and Sages of old felt for, if haply they could find,

and greatly desired, but in vain,

until in the fulness of time all was revealed.

LONDON,
Christmas Day, 1897.

ESSAYS

ON

RELIGIOUS CONCEPTIONS.

I.

THE DAWN OF A RELIGIOUS CONCEPTION.

1. Exordium.
2. Indian.
3. Mesopotamian.
4. Egyptian.
5. Conclusion.

1. *Exordium.*

In the last generation many things were fondly assumed upon very insufficient data, and upon traditional authority, which refused to be brought to the usual literary tests. A hazy, legendary, atmosphere enveloped the origin of all mankind, whether cultured, or barbarous. To the numerically small tribe of the Hebrews was attributed a superiority in things material, as well as spiritual. The people of Egypt, and Mesopotamia, were hardly thought of, except with reference to the very prejudiced character given of them in Hebrew story. We have got beyond that Epoch now: without claiming even now any finality, we see enough to convince us of certain facts:

(1) That the races of mankind, white, yellow, black, brown, and red, did not come from one common ancestor.
(2) That the Languages of mankind did not spring from the same, but very different, and totally distinct, seedplots.

(3) That the Earth was created and peopled by the Human race at a period infinitely in excess of the Four Thousand years conventionally received, as preceding the great Anno Domini, which is the basis of all present calculations.

Nothing is stated, or implied, in this Essay, which would throw doubts on the received tenets of any Religion: they lie entirely outside the present discussion: indeed, the Epoch, included in these remarks, is thousands of years anterior to the Christian era. Two volumes have during the last year been published, which throw light upon the dawn of Religious Conceptions in three countries far distant, and with no intercourse with each other at the remote period, which is described: these books are feelers on scientific principles into the mist, which has originally surrounded the cradle of the Human race: there is no object on the part of the Authors to make false statements, or conceal truths, as is sometimes the case in discussions relating to Religious Conceptions, which still hold sway. In all three cases centuries have elapsed since belief in the Religious Conceptions alluded to, only as a matter of History, has passed away. As a fact, it is only through Religious Legends, and Inscriptions, that we are able to form any opinion of the Conceptions, and ideas, of the Human race in that far-away Epoch. We see clearly, that, however much we may be justified in declaring, that the Hamitic Egyptian, the Non-Arian and Semitic Chaldaeans, and the Arian Indian, did not spring from the same parent, and that their Languages are so totally distinct in principle, as well as structure and vocabulary, as to render a common Linguistic origin impossible; yet we see unmistakably, that these three illustrious races, who have left their indelible footprints on the sands of time, were of the same category of created animals, the genus *Homo*, with the same capacities, tendencies, greatnesses, and weaknesses, the same desire to leave records of themselves to be studied by future ages, the same desire to feel after their Creator, for they had all been endowed with the two congenital gifts of a "Religious Instinct," and "Language-making faculty," differentiating them from the lower animals, because they had an innate conviction of the existence of

"Self," "the World," and an "Unknown Superior Power outside the World."

As a fact, no tribe, however barbarous, has been discovered without the "Language-making faculty," which enabled the "Self" to communicate with his contemporaries, "the World," which the slightest acquaintance brought into evidence, as a feature of daily life: and no tribe, however Savage, which is a degree lower in the scale than barbarous, has not revealed to the inquirer the fact of his having a Religious Instinct, however gross, and undeveloped. But these three great Nations, who form the subject of this Essay, had in the course of centuries advanced far beyond Barbarism, and had learned to erect architectural structures, which will last as long as the great globe lasts, to communicate with all succeeding generations by means of the art of expressing sounds by symbols, which each of the three effected in a totally different way: by means of Ideograms in the case of the Egyptians, of Cuneiform Syllabaries in the case of the Chaldaeans, and of an Alphabet in the case of the Indians. They had conceived out of their own consciousness (waiving, for the sake of this argument, the possibility of a superhuman Inspiration) the most exalted and holy sentiments, the consciousness of a Creator, the idea of a Future State beyond the grave, to which Knowledge the pre-Exilic Hebrew never attained; and they have left behind them, to the admiration, and for the instruction, of future ages, a flow of ideas of imperishable beauty, and a combination of words, which will never die, or cease to charm.

The order, in which the three branches of the subject are treated, has no relation to the question of the earlier, or later, date with reference to each other, which has provisionally been assigned to them: the reader is conducted from the East to the West: from the Doab of the Rivers Ganges and Indus, to the Mesopotamia of the Rivers Tigris and Euphrates in Asia, and the basin of the River Nile in North Africa.

By the word "Ancient" in this Essay a period is assumed anterior to:

(1) The appearance of Gautama Buddha in North India as regards India, say 550 B.C.
(2) The call of Abraham as regards Chaldaea, say 1900 B.C.
(3) The thirteenth Dynasty as regards Egypt, say 1900 B.C.

It has already been stated, that their Languages totally differed, in structure as well as vocabulary, and it is a fact, that the principles, upon which their form of script was based, were diametrically opposed, and, as if to evidence the great versatility of Human powers of invention, the materials, on which the ancient documents have come down to later ages, were totally different.

(1) In India the Veda have come down to us in Manuscript, written by a reed upon perishable material, the leaves of plants, and the date of the oldest survivor of copies of copies is not much anterior to the Norman Conquest of England: there has been room for forgery, intercalation, and emendation of the text.

(2) In Mesopotamia we can handle the original documents in baked clay-bricks in precisely the same state, in which they left the hand of the scribe: there is no room here to doubt the genuineness of the ancient document, however much the correctness of the interpretation of the modern Scholar may be questioned.

(3) In Egypt we can handle the original papyri, and pass our hands across the engraved stelae: if later generations of Monarchs have attempted in some cases to manipulate such documents as the latter, detection is easy: it is not a copy of an original document, but the original document violated by later corrections.

Still more wonderful is the History of these three Nations since the periods, which above have been fixed as the limit of the inquiry:

(1) India remains to this day with the same dominant race, to a certain extent intermixed with immigrants from other parts of Asia, and survivals of races of an earlier settlement in India than themselves. A population of 280 Millions occupies the Regions of Nearer and Further India, and the Indian Archipelago, to which the Culture of Vedic India extends: this makes up nearly one-fifth of the population of the globe. The Religious conceptions of two-thirds of this mass are based on the Veda, and from its bowels have gone forth the first great propagandist Religious Conception of the World, of which Buddha, a Native of India, was the sole founder, and which embraces three hundred additional Millions in the Extreme Orient: thus, fully one-third of the population of the World received its idea of Religion from India.

(2) Of the Culture, the Language, the Religion, of Mesopotamia, the very name had died, and was absolutely extinguished before the time of Alexander the Great; it left no successor to its great inheritance, and no trace of its existence, until the present century had excavated the remnants of its greatness. The supercilious Greek, and Roman, and Arab, knew nothing even by Legend of their great predecessor in Arts, Science, and Arms. It cannot even be said with certainty, that there are any racial descendants of these Mighty Men, who ruled in Mesopotamia, and founded Babylon before the birth of the progenitor of the Hebrew tribe, which has occupied hitherto a place in History so unduly proportioned to its really insignificant existence from a material point of view.

(3) The Individuality, the Religion, the Language, of Egypt, died out gradually a few centuries after the Christian Era; but her name, and her gigantic Monuments, secured to her through all ages

a mysterious place in History, and the undefined influence of her Culture was felt, if not acknowledged, by the races in Europe, springing into existence.

One more distinctive feature in their fate may be laid stress on: our knowledge of India cannot be carried back so far as those of the other two countries, but that knowledge has always been above ground, on the lips of men, and in unbroken continuance up to the present hour. Our knowledge of Mesopotamia can *now* be carried back to an unfathomable antiquity: but there has been an interval of suspended life for centuries; the voice, which now calls to us across the void, sounds like that of a telephone from a distant country. The Greek and Roman marched over the remains of great cities without knowing even their names; yet these cities have now given out of their depths vast libraries. Our knowledge of Egypt can be carried back to a date as remote, but, though little was known of the treasures concealed in her tombs, yet its name and reputation had survived the extinction of the kingdom, Language, and possibly of the race.

We must never lose sight of the fact, that a vast amount of ancient Literature has hopelessly perished. It might be a good argument against the truth of an event, alleged to have taken place in modern times, that there is no allusion to it in contemporary History; but this does not apply to those ancient times, and we must always bear in mind, that the priceless treasures, which haughty Time has spared to us, may be only an inconsiderable fragment of what once existed. We know that several books of the Hebrews have been lost to us, and it is a constant check to our over-confidence to recollect, that more may still be revealed by later excavations. Still, new theories should be cautiously advanced; and those, who now lay stress on the great antiquity of Arabian Inscriptions, and claim for it the honour of being the Parent of Alphabetic writing, as Egypt and Mesopotamia are unquestionably the Parents of Hieroglyphic and Cuneiform respectively, had better hold their breath for awhile, and marshal their evidence, for as a fact, Arabia is not credited with playing any great part in Ancient History. But all things are possible, if we have but the grace to wait.

2. *Indian.*

An interesting volume has lately appeared with the title of "Vedic India," one of the series of the "Stories of the Nations," as embodied principally in the Rig Veda, by Madame Zenaide A. Ragozin, M.R.A.S., author of the story of Chaldaea, Abyssinia, and Persia in the same series, 1895. The Veda, in an archaic Dialect of the Sanskrit Language, is the sole authority: there is no other contemporary Literature. The Science of this subject has been created in the last half-century, and the authoress of "Vedic India" has boiled down the accumulated knowledge of a series of illustrious Scholars into a convenient size.

The old theory of an Arian race is well-nigh exploded: there is unquestionably an Arian, or Indo-European, Family of Languages, but Language is only one, and not the most important, type of a race, and it is quite possible for the same or similar Languages to be used by totally distinct races, distinct in colour, hair, and physical structure. The Arian-Language-speaking Indian race may be considered as a separate race, with strong affinities, to its Iranian neighbour.

The Veda have been always, and are still, emphatically held to be a direct verbal Revelation, communicated to men by the Creator and Ruler of the world. Of their genuineness, and considerable antiquity, there can be no doubt, but there are no materials for carrying back their date to anything like Egyptian or Chaldaean Antiquity. There is no room for fraud or deception in the compilation of the Veda: students may take a different view of the meaning of passages, and of the inductions to be thence made, but this is a matter of scholarship, not of prejudice, partiality, or interested traditional interpretation: there is no room for Higher Criticism here: there is no class, whose stipends and social position in life depend upon the scientific question as to particular documents being written at particular periods by particular men.

For many centuries these volumes, both poetry and prose, were handed down to successive generations orally. At length the time came, at an uncertain period, before the Christian era, but modern when compared to Egyptian or Mesopotamian Records, say 400 B.C., when they were conveyed to Alphabetic writing on perishable materials, subject to all the incidents of errors of copyists. These Books speak for themselves, as they reveal the piety, the intelligence, the poetical genius, and the logical powers, of that ancient race, which found its way across the Hindu Kush into the Panjáb in North-West India, at some remote period.

The number of persons who nominally accept the Brahmanical Conception exceeds two hundred Millions, and with the exception of a few, who are absent in East Africa, or Further India, they all dwell in the vast Region of Nearer India: they speak upwards of one hundred Languages, have created in times past a wondrous Literature, are in the front rank of Commerce, Agriculture, Manufacture, and Science. Strange to say, there is an annual addition to their Religion by voluntary adhesion of Nature-worshipping tribes, and an annual increase of their numbers by the process of generation. There is an infinite number of subdivisions of Castes, and Sects, rendering all intercourse by way of commensality and intermarriage impossible: they represent one-seventh of the population of the round World, and it is impossible to treat them as a negligable quantity, on account of their compact Nationality, their enormous numbers, their wealth, and intellectual capacity.

People in Europe may imagine, that the precise Ritual and dogma of the Veda are believed by the common people now : those, who think thus, forget that Religious Conceptions are Progressive, and are modified and contracted, or develop and expand, according to the influences of the Period, and Environment. We have witnessed in England the birth and progress both of Ritualistic and Evangelical tendencies : the people of India are as far from the tenets of the Veda, as the worldly classes of the people of England are from the Doctrines preached in Galilee. The Hindu has been always tolerant and receptive; and modern Hinduism, like Topsy in the famous Novel, "grew," absorbing much from Non-Arian races, in whose midst it developed. A Book lately published at Allahabad, "Introduction to the Religion and Folklore of North India," by Mr. W. Crooke, confirms this view, which I had long entertained. As regards the common folk, such as those whom the Pharisees in the New Testament cursed as ignorant of the Law, they are quite free from the charge of knowing anything whatsoever of the Veda, Vedanta, Bhágavad Gíta, Puránа, etc., etc.

In the Greek Cosmogony, Demeter represented the rich bounty of Nature in bringing out of the Earth abundant Harvests, by which Life was sustained : what greater Miracle than the Annual Crop springing from the tiny seed? So Dionúsos represents the annually returning clusters of grapes to make glad the heart of man. But to all things belonging to Earth there are limitations : the Sun, Moon, and the Elements are phenomena of the whole World, but the fruits of the Earth are localized, and to Millions the idea of the vine and crops of wheat are unknown. A Primitive People thanked God for annual blessings, but they could only see the Near Horizon.

It is generally asserted, that the Deity created the Human race : the Veda tell us another story, that the Human race evolved the Conception or the existence of a Deity, from their own observation of the features of Nature. The first Triad consisted of Váruna (Οὐρανος), who represented the expanse of Heaven ; Agni (Ignis), the Sun, Lightning, and Fire ; and Indra, the controller of the Atmospheric Elements. Man in his simplicity beheld the Sun, the Moon, and the Planets, who seemed in their course to influence, or at least regulate, the Seasons : they represented a sublime exhibition of Power and Motion. Their regularly recurring orbit seemed to infer the existence of an overruling Power: if that Power could be benevolent to Nature in its entirety, as it clearly was, could it not be so to individuals, and it was therefore deserving of thanks for the Past, prayers for the Present, and hope for the Future, as being powerful to save or destroy. In these Vedic hymns there is a simplicity of thought, the first sobbing and plaintive cry of a Human family in their childhood to their great Author and Controller. It has been well said, that the study of the Sacred Books of each Nation is a Revelation of God to man, and the cultivation of Prayer, real Prayer, constitutes the Revelation of man to God.

Another general belief has grown upon us, that the Deity was immortal, while all that belonged to man passed away: the Veda teach, that the Deity, or groups of Deities, have their day, and pass away, while the Conceptions of the Human race, committed to writing, are practically immortal.

As time went on, the great Hindu race multiplied, and grew strong and wealthy, and their Conception of the Divinity varied with their advancing experience: there has been no interruption in the great stream up to the present year. Another Triad, Brahma, Vishnu, Siva, has long since occupied the highest place, very much as Jupiter, Neptune, and Pluto, pushed aside the elder Deities, and so it must be, till the end comes to the Hindu system, as it did fifteen hundred years ago to the Graeco-Latin Conceptions. Education, Intellectual expansion, contact with other Nations, and unlimited Tolerance, are the sure agents of dissolution of old Conceptions, which are out of touch with the spirit of the age. From their ashes some new Phoenix will arise, for no Religion starts on a *tabula rasa*, but rests on some previous Religious stratum, which can only be reached by Tradition, and is a legacy to younger races from races, which have had their day. In the Sixth century before the great Anno Domini, from the Schools of Brahmanical Philosophy, there came forth from his mother's womb a man, who gave birth to three new Religous elements.

(1) That Theology must be accompanied by the highest possible Morality, and self-denying Purity: the Hebrew up to the time of the Captivity, had not reached that point: immoral kings are but a type of immoral people.
(2) That the "Egoism," the selfish desire to find Salvation for yourself, and let perish all the rest of mankind, must give way to Altruism, and that the greatest virtue and joy were to do good to others, and that the very thought of self was evil.
(3) That Religious Conceptions were no longer restricted to one race, or Nationality, but were Universal, good for all the Human race, and that it was a Duty to publish the Message.

This was a wonderful advance, to which the Egyptians and Mesopotamians had never arrived: it is true, that their existence was cut short about the period, when Buddha came into existence, and that as a fact, the worship of Isis did, to a certain extent, become a propagandist Religion during the years of the decay of the Graeco-Roman system.

We must not rest on the notion, that in the long Vedic Period there was no advancement of Thought, no development of ideas: quite the contrary: the World of Intellect expanded there as elsewhere. There was a greater wealth of Religious sentiment in the time of Antoninus Pius than in the time of Pericles. The Bhágavad Gíta far surpasses the Veda in exalted thought, and even in certain passages in the Bhágavad Purána we detect signs of advancement with the advance of the age.

Nor can it be said with certainty, that nothing preceded the Veda. Among the Books of other Ancient Religions there are portions always of an older date, nearer to the "*Juventus Mundi*," with a more archaic appearance, for there are unmistakable traces of artificial refinement, and of corruption, in some lines of the Veda: it is an after-delusion to place them in the Aurora of Human Thought. Such is the opinion of a very competent authority (Barth, "Revue de Religions," iii, 8, 9).

3. *Mesopotamian.*

I pass into a totally distinct and Semitic World. Here we have a wealth of information, garnered during the last quarter of a century: not theoretic speculations, but positive facts: our treasure is positively in the earthen vessels of burnt clay-bricks, intact, and as they came from the hand of the man armed with the steel stylus: during the last 2,500 years no one would have cared to erase, or add, or alter: would that we had the monuments of Hebrew Literature in the same authentic, and unadulterated form! Oh! that Hosea and Amos, when first the art of Alphabetic writing came into free use, had entrusted their utterances to indestructible clay material, instead of to perishing parchment and papyrus. Job cries out (xix, 23, 24), "Oh that my words were now written! oh that they were printed in a book! That they were graven with an iron pen and lead in the rock for ever!" But he was not a Hebrew, and the date of the Book is scarcely before the Exile.

Maspero, in the three Chapters (VII, VIII, IX) on Chaldaea in his epoch-making "Dawn of Civilization," 1894, collects and tabulates all, that was known of Chaldaea up to the Thirteenth Egyptian Dynasty, at which date the first volume of his Monumental work closes. He was not himself a Cuneiform Scholar, but a labourer in a different field; still, he was able to appreciate, and criticize, and affirm, the statements of the able Scholars, who have spoken *ex cathedrá* on the subject. We find ourselves drawn by a vortex into an Epoch far anterior to anything dreamed of in the Annals of India, or the Extreme Orient. His chapter VII treats of the Creation, the Deluge, the History of the Divinities, the Country of Mesopotamia, the Cities, the inhabitants, and early Dynasties. His chapter VIII sets out the facts of the constitution, and revenues, of their temples; their popular Deities, and Theological Triads; Death and Hades. His chapter IX expounds the constitution of the family, and property, their commerce and industry.

He writes as an outsider, not as the man with a single idea: in fact, his interest is with Egypt, the making of which was accomplished as a kingdom in the Thirteenth Dynasty, including the whole Nile Valley, from the spot where the River received its last tributary, to the sea: Thebes was the Capital: a provisional date may be accepted of 1900 B.C. The period of Isolation was coming to an end: the Nomad tribes were showing signs of restlessness on the frontier: the Power, seated in Mesopotamia, was coming into evidence in Central Syria, and Chaldaea, had imposed her Language and form of script upon West Asia up to the confines of Egypt: the time was approaching, when the Basin of the Nile was to come into collision with the Basin of the Euphrates and the Tigris. Not as yet had Abraham left Ur of the Chaldees to settle in Syria, and found the Hebrew race: it is well to lay stress on this, as owing to the ignorance of our ancestors, the tiny tribe of the Hebrew has been elevated to an importance in History and Geography to which it had no claim.

The Cuneiform Written Character differed materially from Hieroglyphics in principle, and in detail: the same may be said of the Languages used in Chaldaea: the most ancient documents are in the Sumerian or Akkadian of the Ural-Altaic Family, with the agglutinative method; and the later documents are in the Semitic, with the inflective method. The absence of pictorial tablets, as in Egypt, prevent our following the Chaldaeans in their daily avocations and recreations; but the inscribed tablets, having been interpreted by the aid of impartial, unprejudiced Science, free from theological traditional bias, which obscures other fields of research, has revealed the ideas of these ancient men as to the origin of their Deities, and the Creation-story, how Bel Merodach defeated Tiamat, or Chaos, and refashioned the World, earth, sea, and heavens, and created man and animals. Had the tribes of Judah and Benjamin disappeared after the Babylonian Conquest of Judaea, as their cousins of the Ten Tribes disappeared after the Assyrian Conquest of Israel, or had Ezra on the return of the Captives, which event was fraught with the Religious History of the World, after their seventy years at Babylon, not carefully arranged such fragments of the Law and the Prophets, as had survived the destruction of Jerusalem, when temple and tower went to the ground, these Chaldaean documents would have had the monopoly of knowledge of the Human Origins, now ascribed to the Hebrew people.

These Chaldaean records do not fail to give account of everything, that happened since the Creation, and calculate the number of centuries betwixt their own time and that great event. Miracles are not wanting. To a wonderful creature, Oannes, they are indebted for the germ of their Civilization: great cities came into existence: one king, Aloros of Babylon, reigned for a period only to be computed by thousands of years, and the reign of his two successors were even longer: 691,200 years are thus accounted for: Berósus, who lived in the Third century before Christ, some fragments of whose History has survived in quotation by other authors, gives us these details, and justifies the sharp criticism of the Roman on Greek authors:

"Quicquid Grecia mendax
"Audet in historiâ."

As to the relation, which some of these legends bear to Old Testament History, I pass them by, as not suitable to the present discussion: but they are of extreme importance.

The Triads of Deities were:

 First. I. Anu, the Heavens.
    II. Bel Merodach, the Earth.
    III. Ed, the Ocean.

 Second. I. Sin, or the Moon.
    II. Shamsh, or the Sun.
    III. Ramman, or the Genius of the Tempest.

The five planets were Merodach or Jupiter; Ishtar or Venus; Nimb or Saturn; Neigal or Mars; Nebo or Mercury. It is noteworthy, that the names of the days of the week, as used to this day, are derived from the Sun, Moon, and these five Planets. Of the Planets two descended to Earth.

 I. Nebo, who became a Soothsayer and Prophet: he invented clay-tablets, and the art of writing upon them.
 II. Ishtar, the Morning and Evening Star, the Goddess of Love, who attracted the sexes to each other: she had most incongruous characteristics.

The Chaldaeans had not the clear idea of a Future State, possessed by the Egyptians: the tomb, and the mummy, were the engrossing subjects in Egypt. The Chaldaean texts are silent as to the condition of the Soul: the living had no further concern with the dead but to get rid of them: the body must, however, not be left without sepulture: but that was all. Still, there was a "double" analogous to the Egyptian Ka, called Ekimmu, for whom provisions and clothing, ornaments, and arms, had to be supplied: he would then be a guardian to his children. If abandoned, or forgotten, he returned to his home, and tormented his relatives: if not buried, he became a danger to the entire city. At the present day, after the lapse of 5,000 years, the Chinese have not got beyond this stage of Eschatology. Heavy sentences, and frightful punishments, await those, who sinned according to the then prevalent ideas of Sin. Homer and Virgil in their famous Poems caught up the echo of these ideas, and the descent of Orpheus to get back his wife from Tartarus has an analogy in the descent of Ishtar to fetch back Tammuz, or Adonis, which recalls portions of Hebrew and Greek Mythology. It is noteworthy, that the Chaldaean scribe never used the Papyrus, which he could easily have imported from Egypt, nor skins of beasts. Clay-tablets were his only material, whether for home, or foreign, business, as is evidenced by the records lately discovered at Tel al Amarna, or Arsinoe, in Upper Egypt: he had clay-slabs always ready, and a stylus with fine points: later on the end of the stylus was used in the shape of a wedge; hence *cuneus* and "cuneiform."

The two great Basins of the Euphrates and the Nile contained the germ of the Civilization of Western Asia and Europe: they each had their Heaven-appointed spheres, with unlimited power of unopposed expansion, and no bone of vital contention. Neither of them had up to a certain date ventured into the sphere of the other: they had no lack of friendly intercourse, and any chance collision led to no serious results: they were not near enough to hate each other. Ignorance was the great charm against Ambition. In due course of time they did come into a death-struggle, which eventuated in the absolute extinction of the independence of both: Persia, Greece, and Rome, swept their power off the map.

Between these two great Powers, Egypt and Chaldaea, was a miserable buffer-State, destined centuries later to be the most remarkable in the World. Its political position was somewhat analogous to that of Afghanistan at the close of the Nineteenth century, a miserable buffer betwixt the Powers on the Basin of the Oxus, and the Indus. Like Afghanistan, Syria was devoid of Culture, but full of Egoism, and Fanaticism: strange to say, some visionary Ethnologists have found a home for the lost ten tribes of Israel amidst the Pastu-speaking Afghans. The late Bishop of Lahór, Dr. French, distinctly asserted it, but gave no good reasons.

The buffer-State of Syria before Abraham left Haran in Mesopotamia, and crossing the Euphrates founded the Hebrew name, race, and Religious Conception, was a poor country 1900 B.C., and when I traversed it from North to South, nearly 1900 A.D., it was still a poor country, and ever must be so in the eyes of those, who have been trained to recognize the features of a fat country, teeming with the prolific gifts of Nature, and watered by gigantic streams.

It contributed nothing to material Knowledge, the Arts and Sciences of the World, but we now know how much we, the heirs of all the ages, owe to Chaldaea and Egypt: they have, as it were, been roused from their deep slumber: before Greece and Rome came into existence even they were on the warpath of every Human Science, were digging into the virgin soil of Human Knowledge. But, though they flourished for centuries, they were not destined to hand on the lamp in uninterrupted succession to Nations, who came after, at least not ostensibly so: the waters of Lethe closed over them: each had their Chronicler during the Grecian Epoch, Berósus and Manétho, but of their works only fragmentary quotations survive: both countries came under the observation of the Father of History, Herodotus. It was reserved to the Nineteenth century to make known what manner of men they were.

4. *Egyptian.*

I pass from Asia into Africa. Wiedemann writes in his late work on the "Ancient Egyptian Doctrine of Immortality," 1895, that "as far back as Egyptian History has been traced, the people "appear to have been not only in possession of written Characters "(Hieroglyphics), but of National Art and Institutions, and *a* "*complete system of Religion*: we cannot trace its beginnings. In "the earliest glimpses afforded of it by Egyptian Texts it appears "as perfect in all its essential parts; nor were after-times able to "effect much change in it by the addition of new features." In the two previous countries it is admitted, that the early Arians migrated into India from the Regions beyond the Hindu Kush, and that the Chaldaeans received their Civilization from the direction of the Persian Gulf. Of the parent country, whence Egypt derived her knowledge and Culture, we are not informed. A kingdom called Punt, probably Ethiopia, or Arabia, is darkly alluded to, and at one time was the object of her ambition: the Nile flowed to her from those mysterious Southern Regions never destined to be reached until this century.

Maspero remarks, that the oldest Monuments scarcely transport us further than six thousand years before the great Anno Domini, but he postulates a date for the first appearance of the race in the Basin of the Nile of at least eight or ten thousand years. When Abraham, the founder of the Hebrew race, went down into Egypt it had already a History of 4,000 or 6,000 years. There is an extraordinary resemblance of the present inhabitants of Egypt, after the lapse of so many centuries, with the pictures of their ancestors painted on the Monuments. I myself remarked this on my first of many visits to Egypt in 1843.

The Egyptians never arrived at the idea of one, impersonal, yet omnipotent, Ruler of the whole World, and not only of the petty

Basin of the Nile, which made up the whole World to them. Such indeed, owing to their ignorance of History of the past, and of comparative Geography of the contemporary World, was the intellectual position of all the elder Nations before 800 B.C., when the Hebrews ceased to be Monolatrists, and became in very deed Monotheists. Egypt did, indeed, arrive at a most complete Conception of a Future State, and a certainty of Rewards and Punishments after Death. Care was taken of the body of the deceased; his double, or Ka, had to be provided for; his Soul, or Ba, had not to be lost sight of. The dryness of the climate, and the nature of the soil, have preserved all these funereal treasures to our day. It is a solemn sight to look at the very features and the body of the reputed Pharaoh of the Exodus in the Museum at Cairo, and still more solemn is it to wander among the excavated remains of places of sepulture of the honoured dead, who were prepared to appear before the Judge, and had a confident hope of everlasting happiness.

From the teaching of their divine and benevolent Ruler, Thoth, the Egyptians learned Astronomy, Astrology, Music, and Drawing, and the art of Writing, by help of which they immortalized themselves, their manner of life, their Moral and Religious views, their notions of History, Geography, and Politics. Their Language is distinct from any Asiatic Language-Family, and has left only a feeble representative in modern times, dead for oral purposes, but living liturgically in the Koptic. Their form of script is the Hieroglyphic, passing in the course of centuries into Hieratic, and Demotic: it is one of their earliest inventions, one of the greatest wonders of the World, and the great ancestor and exemplar of all the Alphabetic systems, which have made Asia and Europe what they are.

There were two cycles, or systems, of the Egyptian Divinities, representing the opinions of the learned men of Memphis and Thebes, the successive great Capitals of Egypt, and marking the progress, as time went on, of the Human Intellect. The two systems were but variations of the same central idea: there were male deities, with most of whom were associated female deities, holding inferior place, except in the case of Isis: one group may be called that of Osiris, one of Ra: the latter group was wholly Solar; the Osiris group consisted of Osiris, his consort Isis, and his opponent Seth. Horus was the child of Osiris and Isis. As in India and Chaldaea, the Egyptian Deities were frequently associated in Triads. Osiris was essentially the " good principle," and in perpetual warfare with the " evil principle." For a time he was vanquished and killed, but came again to life: Horus, his son, avenges his father: the power of the evil principle is destroyed, but not annihilated. Osiris thus became the type of Humanity, its struggles, its sufferings, its temporary defeat, and its final victory: the dead were identified with him, and under the name of Osiris, whether male or female, passed into Amenti, the Divine World below. Here we touch on one of the secrets of Human life and death, and after the lapse of thousands of years have still to walk by faith, not by sight. Moses, though learned in all the wisdom of the Egyptians, was either ignorant of, or purposely reticent on, the subject of a Future State, in those Laws, which are attributed to him, and which he enacted 2,500 years later: much of the Decalogue appears in the famous "Book of the Dead" of the Egyptians, which is of a much earlier date than the Exodus.

No thoughtful person can think lightly of the Religious Conceptions of these great races: they felt after God, if haply they could find Him: if success crowned their efforts in War or Peace, they thanked their Deities, Ashur, or Amen Ra, for his assistance. They were indeed deficient in many essentials of Religion, which after ages taught their successors; but the Eschatological Conceptions of the Egyptians from the earliest time were indeed wonderful. We have only to compare the questions, which the dead were prepared to reply to, and the answers inscribed on papyrus Rolls in Hieroglyphics, which were placed in the Mummy-cases with the dead body, with the sentiments of contemporary and later races, to feel how superior were Egyptian notions upon this material point. Supposing that no portion of the evidence alluded to in this Essay had escaped the rude hand of Time, and come under our eyes, how imperfect would our opinion have been of the moral and intellectual state of our predecessors in the work of Civilization of Mankind!

5. *Conclusion.*

We must think gently of the older World, of our predecessors in the great progress of the Human race. God's poor children were ever what their environment made them: if we doubt this, we in our Nineteenth-century arrogance, and the narrow orbit of our Theological Shibboleth, question the Wisdom and Love of the great Creator, who hates nothing, that He has made. The early occupants of the great Globe, scattered on vast plains, or herding together in great forests, saw the Sun, and the Heavenly Host, and bowed down to them: they were insensibly conscious of the revolution of the Seasons: they saw the war of the elements, and mighty trees torn up by the winds, and great streams blocked up by ice and snow. Around them was an environment of majestic wonders, and they surveyed it sometimes with feelings of thankfulness, sometimes in fear and agony, for the unknown Power seemed to their limited understandings as very capricious: they knew nothing of the unchanging Love of the great Creator, and, when they writhed under famine or pestilence, or the spoliation of men and beasts, they thought, that the great Power was angry, and tried in their weak way to conciliate Him. Not as yet were men congregated in cities; not as yet had they come under the great curse of a Priesthood living by the Sacrificial altar, and in the name of God preaching lies, and setting an example of Pride and Self-will, justifying the scathing line of Lucretius, when he commented on the fact that Agamemnon sacrificed the life of his own daughter under the compulsion of Priests:

"*Tantum Religio potuit suadere malorum.*"

Intolerance, Persecution, Egotism, Fanaticism, and Superstition, caused the Conception of the Relation of the Soul to God to be converted into one of the great curses of the Human race.

Nature-Worship, or as it is now scientifically called the Animistic Conception, or Spirit-Worship (miscalled Devil-Worship by the ignorant Missionary), was the first round in the great ladder, by which the Soul of man, in fear and trembling, in deep debasement and hopeless ignorance, felt its way to the acknowledgment, and Worship, of the great unknown Power, to which it felt, that it owed its existence, its preservation, and its Future. The heart of man, even in his deep degradation, turns to its Maker as the sunflower turns to the Sun.

All Human affairs exist only by the force of Evolution and Development. In the absence of this onward influence they die. So in its appointed time in a tribe of Nature-Worshippers there appears a man, greater than his contemporaries, with the power of looking forward into the Future. He collects and arranges all the oral legends of his tribe: if a power of writing exists in his Epoch, he commits them to writing: he dares to legislate for the Future. Among such men were Moses, Zoroaster, Confucius, the Hindu Sages, and Pythagoras, Socrates, Plato.

II.

The Decay of a Religious Conception.

1. Exordium.
2. Egyptian.
3. Mesopotamian.
4. Graeco-Latin.
5. Conclusion.

1. *Exordium.*

Everything relating to men is subject to the inexorable Law of Decay and Death: their bodies, their material constructions, their intellectual aspirations, their customs, their form of speech, their mode of writing, and lastly their Conceptions as to "Self, the World, God," which make up their environment, varying from century to century, and Region to Region. Our thoughts on this occasion are restricted to the last of the three features of "*la pauvre Humanité*": it is the one, in which they appear to the highest advantage, and also in the deepest degradation.

In my contribution to the International Oriental Congress at Geneva, 1894, published in the English and French Languages, I stated in detail the Religious Conceptions of the Ancient World before the great Anno Domini, both those that have perished, and those that still survive. It is a subject to be treated with solemn reverence, for those ancient men were feeling after God, and the great Creator had not forgotten His poor Children. In my Volume published in 1895 on the "Common Features of all Religious Conceptions," I pointed out the identity of the superficial structure of all, for all sprang from the same innate goodness, and congenital weakness, of the Human race. God looked down from Heaven on all, and was present in all the ages and in all places. Let me now approach philosophically and impartially the causes, which lead to the changes of a Religious Conception. It is too obvious a feature in History to doubt, that changes do take place. The Religious Conception of a people becomes degraded into a spider's web spun by gross and ignorant men for the purpose of hiding God from the community, by Human inventions, and Human word-spinning: by His Grace they have passed away like the clouds in the Sky, and will continue to pass away, while the Sun still remains in the heavens.

Let me clear away prejudices. In the dawn of a Religious Conception men were isolated; in the decay they have come into contact with their neighbours: I boldly state, that it is the same God, by whatever name known, in whatever fashion worshipped, who created the whole World, and all that dwell in it. I thank Paul for quoting, and making his own and ours for ever, the words of two Heathen Poets, Cleanthes and Aratus:

"Τοῦ γὰρ γένος ἐσμεν."

He does not love one race more than another, and He hateth nothing that He hath made, whatever Egotistic Hebrews, or ill-instructed so-called Christians, may assert.

He never sanctioned Crime, such as Abraham proposed, and Jephthah and Agamemnon believed, that they were ordered to commit. He never sanctioned spoliation, and wholesale slaughter, such as the Hebrews committed in the invasion of Palestine, or the slaughter of the Priests of Baal by Elijah. He never leaves immorality unpunished, such as that of Solomon or David: in fact, He was all-Wise, Good, Powerful, Holy, Everlasting, Universal, Just, Merciful: all Nations and Tribes have recognized the same invisible Power, and rendered to Him Worship, however imperfect, insufficient, and absolutely wrong, and mistaken, and under different Names. A change of Conception, and Cult, did not entail a change of God. Men in their foolishness, yet piety, in their weakness, yet strength, saw dimly, yet they desired to see and understand the dealings of God, and men in the Nineteenth century see dimly still.

For it is merely opinion supported by Faith, the Πίστις of the New Testament, the Ἐλπις of Socrates, the Emún of the Hebrew, the Bhakti or Biswas of the Hindu, the Imán of the Mahometan, entirely unsupported by external or material Proof, sufficient to satisfy the Intellect, though all-sufficient for the Soul: the receiver of the new Conception can give no reason for it: *it is there, and he will die for it.* We must clear away the barnacles, which cling to the decaying vessel of the old Conception, however venerable: the evil inheritance of ancestral Traditions, which have obscured and shut out of sight the Divine Message, given in the appointed place, at the appointed time, and for the appointed season; the curse of a Priesthood, whether hereditary, or co-opted, whose means of existence depend on the maintenance of an effete and corrupted Shibboleth; the foolishness of National, Tribal, or even Family, Monopoly-Conceptions; the slavery to Words, meaningless Words, which have caused, and may cause again, the wicked shedding of blood of God's poor creatures: whatever may be the errors of the early Conceptions, they were tolerant, if themselves left alone, or expanded peacefully. To Christianity the World is indebted for the idea of Intolerance, Persecution, Propagation by force: Islam succeeded to the baneful inheritance.

It is obvious, that there were survivals of the old Conception in the layers of each new Conception, some of the sad, yet Human, practices of the previous and defunct one. When the time of decay comes, it is found, that there remain important survivals, based on the carnal hopes and ideas of the whole Human race: they passed from the old Epoch, and the *nidus* of the old Nature-Religion, though it had developed into a Book-Religion of Ritual and Liturgy, and passed on into the later and presumably the Spiritual Conception of a more advanced Epoch; for there is no possibility of a retrograde step in the process of Human development. Fetishism and Totemism found their way into the Egyptian Conception, and the Hindu system, an inheritance from African and Pre-Arian races: thus, in the practice of European Christian Churches there are gross survivals of Graeco-Roman Paganism and Judaism. Human customs and dominant ideas become blended with quasi-Religious, so-called Religious, sanctions. The daily pressure upon mankind of Life and Death, Food and Hunger, in the narrow environment of a tribe of low Culture; the low designs of crafty Priests, who live by their altar and its offerings: all these things shut out the believers, the sincere believers, from a clear view of the great Problem working out before their eyes in the gradual intellectual advancement of the Human race, and the full appreciation by the Soul of its relation to the Creator and Preserver of its life. My subject is:

(1) The approaching decay of Religious Conceptions, good for past days, when the round World was partitioned off into Regions entirely separated from each other, with a population in a low state of Culture.
(2) The development of new Religious Conceptions, suited to the Epoch, universal, yet speaking to each individual Soul, based on universal Laws of Morality.

Every period of History has its own perplexities, every generation has its own problem to solve, for the affairs of men disperse, shift, and rearrange themselves, like the bits of glass in a revolving kaleidoscope: things, although familiar enough *in situ*, present themselves in a new aspect when *in motu*. Take for instance into consideration the view of sacred things held in the first year of the Nineteenth century A.D. and contrast it with the view taken now: who would venture in the pulpit of the current year to preach a sermon of that period? From generation to generation the point of view varies even in the case of the most ordinary Religious Conception? Reform, and fresh adaptations, are called for, and meet the necessity, but in the elder World the whole of the ancient machinery had to be swept away, generally by violence, and place made for a new structure.

The Roman Empire openly and avowedly admitted the Religious Conceptions of all subject Nations into their cities, on the condition, that they respected each other, that, being allowed to live, they let others live: but this is just, what the Christians of that period never would do: they were ever committing some sacrilegious act, or refusing to comply with some purely municipal requirement, in order to obtain Martyrdom. No sooner had they got the upper hand than they came out as intolerant persecutors: the Temple of Jerusalem was destroyed by the Romans, as an accident of a siege for political purposes, but the Temple of Serápis at Alexandria was deliberately destroyed by Christian Intolerance. Nothing of this kind has taken place, or could take place, in British India. This marks the total difference of the environment, and places a new problem before our eyes.

It is so seldom, that a Religious Conception has been allowed to die away by a natural death: its last moments have ordinarily been troubled by the fanatical advocates of the new Conception, as instanced in the last years of the Graeco-Roman System, and the treatment of Animistic Conceptions everywhere. It will be a new incident in the History of the World to watch the peaceful decay, or gradual transformation, of the Brahmanical, Buddhist, and Confucian, Conceptions, while the Powers of the World stand by, and keep the lists open.

But even though the arrogant intolerance of the Persecutor is restrained, there are more powerful antagonists in the field, who were formerly quite unknown: (1) Education, (2) Civilization, (3) Contact with other Nations, (4) Commerce and Travel. It was the absence of every one of these four factors, that made the Hebrews before the Captivity such a peculiarly odious and priggish fourth-rate Nation, objects of scorn to the professors of the Egyptian and Babylonian Conceptions, although both of them had certain extinction coming upon them at the hands of the Persian followers of Zoroaster, and the Greek Disciples of Aristotle and Plato.

Then, again, if the agents of Conversion were content to offer the pure simple tenets of the Founder of the new Conception, the transformation would have been easier, but down to the present Epoch the new doctrine is always presented in a deformed, and hardened, exterior, rendered distasteful by the local accretions of some particular Nationality. The words of the Teacher of Galilee were good for, and acceptable to, all mankind, in all climes, all degrees of Culture, every variety of environment; but the folly of mankind elects to present it to the Hindu and Chinese in the disguise of an English middle-class specific, or an American, or German, newly invented Prescription.

When a Religious Conception is in decadence, as the consequence of its own emptiness, like an exhausted volcano, supposing that there is an entire absence of the Arm of the Flesh, and Intolerance, phenomena are generally found of the following kind: Those, who are advanced in life, or conservative in temperament, or grossly ignorant, or fanatically devoted to the expiring Conception, or really and truly believing in it, or dependent on it for their daily bread, such as Priests and Ministers, generally divide themselves into three factions:

(1) Those, who attempt to elude notoriety, and conceal their Religious convictions, playing the part of hypocrites.
(2) Those, who in theory respect their ancient Beliefs, but being hopeless conform to some new one, and thus preserve their social position.
(3) Those, who retire from the world into voluntary exile for the sake of their Faith, and resign all outward practice of the old Cult.

We can imagine something of this kind at the time of the Reformation in England until all the old Romish Priests had died out, or left the country. Even then many a decaying old man or old woman must have clung to their last hour to their "Ave Maria" and the husk of a Religious Conception, which was all that the Romish Priest had taught them. And as time goes on, and the contemporaries of the great Transformation die out, the thoughts of the new generation widen with the lapse of years. We should look at the matter with a practical and philosophic eye. Does the stupid conservative not feel, that it is the same God, who rules all the World at all times, and that the great intellectual, and spiritual, movement of the Nineteenth century is as much His gift, or as much permitted by him, as the imperfect Physical, Intellectual, and Spiritual, half-knowledge of the Third century, or the overbearing dogmatism of the Dark Ages. The great Truth in Christ does not require the support of Anathemas, or Pulpit-exaggerations, or "My-Doxy" assumptions; nor does Faith in Christ necessitate the hiding of the believer's head like an ostrich in the sand.

The marks of a decaying Religious Conception are:

I. Leaning on the Arm of the Flesh, and Intolerance.
II. Clinging to the original or Translation of some Book of elder ages: Worship of the letter instead of the Spirit.
III. Maintaining an intolerant, unsympathetic, and ignorant Priesthood, whose bread would be jeopardized by any change.
IV. Abstaining from all attempts to convey the so-called Truths, and Precious Promises, of their Conceptions to the outer World.

V. Enforcing strict Rules of Caste as regards Marriage and Commensality.
VI. The Arts of Sculpture and Painting are dangerous allies to a pure Spiritual Conception of the Infinite and Indescribable. They are the sure forerunners of a secret Idolatry: the old man in the Clouds represents the Creator; the beautiful young woman in a purple dress with an infant represents the Virgin Mother; the Dove represents the Holy Ghost. The poison of Anthropomorphism clings to a falling Conception.

2. *Egyptian.*

It is placed beyond doubt, that at a period of its Natural life so remote that it is difficult to state it, as it is totally prehistoric, the Egyptian settlers in the Basin of the Nile possessed a Religious Conception of a most elaborate, exalted, and spiritual, nature. The Soul of man was recognized as totally distinct from the body: the latter might perish, but the former never: and there was a Day of Judgment, and those, who had passed good lives, were not only in the presence of Osiris, but were identified with Osiris. The Sovereigns and their subjects had the strength of their convictions, and raised up mighty structures, which exist to this day, and tell their own story. The art of writing, as the name "Hieroglyphic" indicates, was invented for sacred purposes, and made use of to an extraordinary extent. Great and Holy Thoughts, and everlasting Truths, were committed to these writings, and haughty Time has been just, and spared them. The same leading phenomena developed themselves, the Conception of a Trinity of the three great Deities, of the death of a son, Osiris, for the benefit of mankind: there came into existence Sacred Books, Priesthoods, Ritual, Belief in a Judgment after Death, and Rewards or Punishments. In the last generation the Egyptians had the reputation of having been savage idolators, who behaved shamefully to the worthy and excellent descendants of the Hebrew shepherd Jacob, who condescended to dwell in their country. A different view is entertained now. Still, the singular fact remains, that a period was fixed by the Most High to the Religious Conception of the Egyptians: there were no seeds of permanence: they lasted three or four thousand years, then fell into decadence under the rule of the Persian Conquerors, and disappeared under the rule of the Macedonians, leaving no successor to inherit their accumulated Wisdom, and their developed Ritual, for by a freak of fortune the whole Religion, Language, and Form of Writing, were enveloped in a sudden darkness, and buried out of sight in the bowels of the earth, leaving no trace in the worship of those who succeeded them.

It died, and left no influence on the Religious Conception, which succeeded it.

It is remarked by a thoughtful writer that "Egyptian Civiliza-"tion (including the Religious Conception) was complete and fully "developed, but, like that of China, was not on the main line of "Human Progress, and consequently left little or no influence "on future centuries." (P. Gardiner, "New Chapters in Greek History," p. 193.)

Another writer remarks with regard to the Egyptian Religious Conception in its latest form, when Serapis had become an object of Worship to Greeks and Romans as well as to Egyptians:

"All my reading convinces me, that a satisfactory exegesis of "Pagan Religious Conceptions is given only by those writers, who "believe, that the earliest Religious ideas of the Human race were "derived from man's daily observation of the awe-inspiring cosmical "phenomena. The primary notion was, that the life-giving, light-"bearing Sun, was the greatest of Natural and Divine things, "'the One Great over All.' He was the Boat, that conveyed the "Dead to the next World, the Ruler of the Day, the Ray-crowned "King of the World." (Palestine Exploration Quarterly, Oct., 1896, p. 338.)

It is obvious that increased knowledge of the Universe, and contact with other Nations, would dissipate this idea, and the Religious Conception built upon so unsolid a base would disappear: this is too simple an explanation. Mystery is required, Legends, Glamour (shall we say Falsehood?) are required, to maintain a Religious Conception, for the Human race is so foolish on such subjects, that it lends faith to any solemn well-compacted Lie.

3. *Mesopotamian.*

They were but one branch of the great Semitic Family. The course of the Egyptian Religious Conception had been, like their own River Nile, a solitary one, receiving no affluents from other Nations, pouring itself into no great sea. The same may be said of the Mesopotamian Religious Conception. The great Persian and Graeco-Latin Conceptions crushed out its life, and after the lapse of twenty-four centuries we can only dimly trace out what was the belief of those ancient men, and this has been described in the preceding Essay. It had no influence on succeeding ages: it left no great successor to occupy new ground, in the way in which the Brahmanical Conception gave birth to the Buddhist Conception, and the Hebrew Conception to the Christian and Mahometan Conceptions.

4. Graeco-Latin.

It may be asserted with truth, that under the Roman Empire a total eclipse took place of the Religions of Egypt and Mesopotamia. The waters of Lethé passed over them, and not by violent oppression, or Missionary teaching, but by their own weight they sank, unvalued, forgotten, despised. Such was not the case of that beautiful Conception, which prevailed in Greece and Rome during the Epoch of their greatest glory. Though in the Languages of the two Nations every god and goddess had a different name, yet they were clearly identical, and made up a great part of the Greek and Roman life, appearing in their Literature, in their customs, in their words, in their statuary. The veriest schoolboy knows all about the great Trinity of the Graeco-Latin Religious Conception:

(1) Zeus or Jupiter: the Father, the Creator, the Controller.
(2) Phoebus Apollo: the Son, the Lord of Light, and Healing.
(3) Athene or Minerva: the Holy Spirit, who sprang from the brain of the Father, and who was ever at the side of her worshippers.

The great oath of the Greeks was:

"Ναὶ μὰ Ζεῦτε πάτερ, καὶ 'Αθηναίη, καὶ 'Απόλλον."

HOMER'S *Iliad*.

Demeter or Ceres, Dionúsus or Bacchus, Ares or Mars, Hermes or Mercury, Aphrodite or Venus, all are familiar to every schoolboy, and their names live after they have been deposed, for Poetry and Sculpture have cast an everlasting halo round them.

Why did they die? They were merely deified mortals, with like passions, lusts, hatred, envy, jealousy, as men, and they were crushed by the common-sense of the two most intellectual races of mankind: it was not by the arm of the intolerant persecutor, but by the weight of their own spiritual inadequacy, that they fell. The great Dramatists of Athens, the Philosophers of the different Greek Schools, the wisest and greatest of Roman Philosophers and Poets, all contributed to their downfall. It is not sufficiently dwelt upon, how exceedingly opportune as regards place and time was the appearance in the midst of the Human race of the Son of God, for three short years, *three short years only*, and yet the environment of Culture, and Human politics, was ready, as it has never been before or since, to receive Him. No reader of the poetry of Lucretius, of Horace, Virgil, and Juvenal, of the writings of Cicero, Seneca, Marcus Aurelius, and Epictétus, can fail to remark, that there was a change coming over the minds of men of the Latin race, that they had outlived the Religious Conceptions of their ancestors. The stupid conservative of that period, just as the same stamp of men at other periods, attributed the downfall of Rome to the neglect of the worship of the gods, who had made Rome great, but we know well, that the rise and fall of Nations does not depend on their Religious Conceptions.

Still more marked were the circumstances of the Greek people. The Oracle of Delphi was ceasing to be trusted. Education, and the diffusion of Literature, were having the same powerful effects in Greece, which they are now having in British India. The legendary tales, which had satisfied past generations, did so no longer. The great dramatist, Euripides, lived at an Epoch, when the Olympian gods were preparing to depart: after the death of Socrates *they did depart*. The legends of Hellas were brought to the crucible of the wit, the inuendo, the suggestion, of the free-thinking Dramatist. Consider the plot of such a Drama as that of "Alcestes": can anything be conceived more ridiculous than that of a woman after her death being dragged back from her grave by a strong hero such as Hercules, who seized Death, while he was eating the funeral offerings, and compelled him to surrender his prey? If the legends of King Arthur were treated in this Human fashion, or the legends of the Old Testament, would they outlive the ridiculous *impasse*, at which they had arrived? There was no public Press in Greece, as there is now in India; but the Theatre and the Schools of Philosophy did the work of public inquiries: they asked the reason why, and compelled the reader and hearer to ask themselves, whether what was stated could be true. A fabulous legend translated into the facts of contemporary life, prosaic life, composed of the incidents of life, sickness, and death, must shrivel into nothing, like a bladder that is pricked.

The Drama was not only a part of the Annual Festival, but it was an advertisement of it: the subject of the Drama became the staple subject of the current Literature of a public beginning to indulge in private reading: it was only at the close of the Fifth Century before Christ, that the rapid growth of intellectual power, taught the public the advantage of private reading, or reading aloud, and this proved one of the dissolvents of the age. A similar process is going on in British India now. Reading led to conversation, discussions, and the desire to hear something new. Thus the Greek World was unconsciously preparing itself for the reception of a new Idea, a new intellectual and spiritual environment. Philosophy, and Ridicule, and Common-sense, had stamped out the supernatural myths of an earlier age. Something newer, fresher, more suited to the Epoch, was required: and in the fulness of time it came.

There was a *stupid* party there as elsewhere, and they would have liked to go on believing in the legend of Alcestes, as in the miracle of some mediaeval Saint; but the impetus of the spirit of the new age was too great, and the whole visionary fabric disappeared like a dream. Such will ever be the fate of any Religious Conception, which is allowed to fall behind the Epoch, and the intellectual standpoint, of the worshipper. Such was it when, centuries later the degraded Christian Churches in Western Asia and North Africa fell before the lofty Monotheism of Islam.

An an illustration of the above I quote passages from Bishop Boyd Carpenter's "Narcissus":

"The conversation would turn upon the faith, which Drusilla "held, and upon the gods, to which the mother of Felix still clung "with a reverent fondness. Her temperament was that of one, "who fears to let slip her faith; her whole heart was bound up in "her home; she dreaded the wrath of the gods, because she feared "lest any change should rob her of what she prized so highly, "her little Felix and her husband. Her pleasant home and its "warm love were to Valeria her all in all; and she would have "embraced any faith, which would secure the favour of any deity, "and so preserve her household happiness." (pp. 6, 7.)

"There [at Athens, Felix] had learned to look with broader "thought upon these beliefs; for he had met with various faiths, "and all, in a measure, had something to commend them, and the "gods of Olympus were at least deifications of truths, powers, and "qualities, and, if he could not worship them, he could admire the "qualities and powers; and, perhaps, it was as well to let the "weaker and more ignorant go on in their worship of the gods "themselves. Indeed, for anything he knew, there might be "something of truth in their worship. At least, he would "hardly like to let go the poetry of paganism." (p. 61.)

Here opens out the great problem of Religious Conceptions: it seemed to be a question of the Epoch of the individual.

5. *Conclusion.*

A time surely comes, when men learn the art of Intercomparison; and the worshippers of what appeared to one particular tribe unique, learn to their surprise, that the Religious Conception, which they thought was made for them and them alone, really was the property of the Human race, that all mankind was equally endued with a desire to find, and a power to search for, the great Author of their existence. The Hebrew race talked, and still talk, of *their* Jehovah: they were at first monolatrists, not monotheists, but they gradually rose to the conviction, that Jehovah was Lord of the whole of creation, including the few thousands of Israel

It is all very well to build for eternity, and to keep repeating the words "for ever," but it is a truth, that old forms wear out, old ideas become obsolete, old words lose their meaning. We may thank God, that the progress of the Human race is ever onward, and upward, and that there is progress all down the line. In the decay of a Religious Conception, the Priests are generally in fault: they live by their altar; they cannot see that the environment, and the point of view, are changing and expanding. As a rule the conservative party is stupid, selfish, incapable of self-sacrifice, and impotent to mark the progress of the Human Intellect. The Priests encourage esoteric Worship: they place stress on Ritual, observance of times, places, seasons, and old-fashioned ideas of the great Kosmos: they, in fact, become themselves carnal, ignorant, intolerant, and ready to appeal to the Arm of the Flesh. It is clear, that in a certain stage of every Religious Conviction degeneracy sets in: the height of lofty Conception has been theoretically attained, but there is a limit. Then carnality sets in: Myths obscure the Truth; words are used for the purpose of hiding rather than expressing meaning; cruel and even immoral rites take the place of old simple forms. As in the trees of the forest, so in the individuals of a great race, we can watch the progress of the birth, youth, maturity, senility, decay, and death: so is it with Religious Conceptions; they have their day and disappear: the reason is, that the wave of progress is always in motion: we see the face of Nature always changing; we see generations of men pass from the cradle to the grave, we cannot expect to find permanence in what by nature is so fickle and mobile as the ideas of man with regard to things totally invisible, intangible, and inconceivable. In a book published at Calcutta, "An Introduction to the Study of Hinduism," by Guru Prosád Sen, I read the opinion of the author, " that Hinduism is not, and never has been, a *Religious* organization: " it is a purely social system, exacting from the Hindu the observance " of certain social forms, and not the profession of a particular " Religious Belief: the Hindu may choose to have a faith and " creed, if he wants one, or do without one: so long as a man holds " to his Caste he may even accept the doctrine of Christianity." Has not conventional Christianity fallen to this level also? Christianity has become a social association, entirely free from any speculative thought, or rational belief: is it not in both a sign of decay?

Only let the transition be gentle, and not marked by cruelty: let us consider the lesson read to us by the treatment of the temple and image of Serápis at Alexandria, and the conduct of Christian Emperors, Bishops, and the savage, ignorant monks of Alexandria. Let the idol fall by its own weight from its pedestal, and the temple disappear in ruins by natural decay, or stand like the Parthenon, and the temple of Balbek, as an architectural voice from the Past. Let us only imagine the Missionary Societies, and the crafty religious fanatics of the middle-classes in great Britain, getting the upper hand in Banáras or Amritsar, and the streets flowing with blood, and the Brahmins slaughtered by a new crop of Elijahs, in the name of the Message of Peace, Forgiveness of Sins, Pity, Pardon, and Love. What a much higher triumph it would be to see the miracle-working statue, the Holy Coat, and the bones of departed Saints, transferred voluntarily to the Museum of Antiquities, and to leave the bats in the possession of the deserted temple!

The decay of a Religious Conception is indeed not Death, but Transition to some higher Form of Belief in the great Controller of the Universe, some sweeping away of empty Forms, and attempt of the poor worshipper to approach nearer to the object of his Worship. When a Religion of the elder type, attached to some particular Region, built up on Legends, supported by assertions of Visions and Miracles, symbolized by Sacrifice of Beasts and Birds, has run its course, or fallen into deep degradation, ever and anon there comes a man like Hosea (800 B C.) crying out: "Come, and let us return unto the Lord, for I desired mercy and not sacrifice, and the knowledge of God more than burnt-offerings" (vi, 1, 6). We see through all the ages since that initial date a succession of such men, dauntless, eloquent, reasoning with their countrymen: Buddha, Socrates, Paul, Mahomet, Luther, Calvin, Kabír, Nának, Wesley. God has not left Himself without a witness. He has been immanent in all the ages, rising up early, and calling, here a little, there a little. Sometimes there came a partial refreshing, and a hand pointing backwards or forwards, according to the period in the History of Man: once in all the ages in the fulness of time the Son of God Himself appeared for three short years out of all the centuries of years before and since, and drew a dividing-line between the Past and the Future. All the old-fashioned paraphernalia of Worship disappeared, such as Oracles, Prophecy, Miracles, Signs from Heaven, Theophanies, and man was taught to worship God in spirit, and be content with the Invisible Presence of the Holy Spirit in each one of us, who does not drive Him from our hearts.

It must be an awful struggle for a conscientious person to change his views on a subject so solemn, to annihilate all the feelings, hopes, fears, loves, hates, of his childhood, and adopt new ones; to feel the pain of family-feuds, and lost friendships: but the great mass of mankind did not believe *much* formerly, nor do they believe *much* now: they merely change an outward garment, seen by the eyes of men, and hiding the nakedness below. In the first period the Religious Conception has come unconsciously: it has grown with the growth of the tribe. In the second period, when one Conception is taking the place of another, there is a struggle, a fierce conflict, a disruption of families, a civil war, and martyrdom. Much is said about Martyrs, as it is about Faith: we must learn always to ask the speaker to tell us for what cause the Martyrdom is undergone? In what invisible Saviour is the Faith?

And too much should not be made of Martyrdom: much depends upon the character of the Martyr. From a book called "Rome and the Early Christians," I select the following extract: "In

" comparison with Labour and Duty it is easy to suffer : compared
" to lifelong labour and duty it is a light service : perhaps in many
" a conflict with temptation and sin, a harder conflict has been
" fought, a harder victory won, than when the flames consumed
" him and the beasts tore him limb by limb. Suffering and dying
" for a Faith is no evidence of the Truth of that Faith. Many have
" died for what others deem *false* Religion : it is a proof, not of
" the Truth of the cause, for which the man or woman died, but of
" their sincerity and dogged determination. Some of the meanest
" characters have made the best martyrs ; some most noble have
" shrunk from infirmity of temperament from the trial."

Again, when a Nation has risen to greatness under what they deem the protection of their National Deities, their poor weak hearts cleave to them : the Worship may be wrong or even injurious, still it is the Religion of themselves, their ancestors, and the *Religio loci*. The feeling is not an unworthy one : the thoughts are raised from low material wants to the Invisible Power, and the inscrutable Future.

Those, who are in middle life, may well ask : " is the new Conception a better one ?" Those, who are low in Culture are scarcely fit judges of what is right : they cannot open out the great question, " Why was I born ? whence do I come ? whither do I go ? for what purpose did I come into life ?" They received the precious gifts of life, and reason, and Language, and a desire to seek after a Power greater than themselves. One thing only is certain, that, as men advance in Culture, they advance in power to appreciate what is holy and right in itself, and to feel sure, that the Divinity must be holy and pure. They unconsciously approach nearer to God.

Even a confessedly imperfect Religious Conception is better than a plunge into Atheism, Agnosticism, Materialism, casting off all idea of a Divine Power. It is well, that men should not change their views on Divine Things without thought, searching of heart, and inquiry. We know too well how an African tribe, like the Ba-Ganda, or the Maori of New Zealand, may be tempted by a sudden impulse, and the prospect of material advantage, to accept a new Idea, and then, when another wave comes over the land, it is found, that their convictions have no firm rest in the heart: they changed once, they are ready to change again: hundreds of so-called Christian converts disappear, or join some other herd, some new wind of doctrine, the enticements of some new Preacher. Where there is a great light, there must be of necessity a great shadow. " *Quieta non movere*," may be a good maxim in Human affairs, but in Divine matters there must be always a sound of motion, for stagnation is fatal to spirituality.

It has fallen to the lot of some to witness, or share, the grief of Parents, whose child has joined the Church of Rome, or become a Mahometan, whose daughter has fallen so far as to be the additional wife of a Mormon; or to openly deny the Atonement, as being unaware of having sins to be atoned for, refusing to be married by any Religious ceremony, or to bring their children to the Baptismal font. It is singular, but the fact is, that even nominal Christians shrink from such conduct, as there is a certain social fashion in favour of certain ceremonies connected with birth, marriage, and death.

All men to a certain extent are on the same platform as regards things spiritual. Religion in modern days is no longer a matter to be controlled by physical force, like a conquered kingdom, or as a scientific problem, such as the discovery of a new planet, or as a matter of evidence such as a case in a Court of Law; for in very deed it is a matter of Faith, the evidence of things not seen, and ἐῶρον Οέου, the gift of God. Paul was the first and greatest of Missionaries. He announced himself to be by divine appointment Apostle to the Gentiles. He had not been set apart by the Lord as an Apostle, or co-opted by them as the twelfth apostle. He declared his own Commission, and gave no proofs but his own word. Without the formality of Council or consultation he set at naught the so-called Law of Moses: he admitted the existence of a Religious feeling, the groping after God, in all mankind. Being fluent in the Greek Language, and a member of the Diaspora in a no mean Greek city in Asia Minor, we might have expected that in arguing about fundamentals, the existence of one sole God, Lord of the whole World, the plan of Salvation through a Mediator, the last Day of Judgment, the Beauty of Morality, he would have fortified his argument by quoting largely from the Dramatists and Philosophers of Athens, showing that Him, whom they ignorantly worshipped, He preached: but he contents himself with one quotation each from Cleanthes and Aratus: he could never forget that he was a Hebrew, though a Hebrew, who deliberately set aside the Law of Moses, quoting from the Scriptures, of which his Gentile hearers had no knowledge whatever. The Modern Missionary in India and elsewhere does just the same: he quotes the Christian Scriptures; he ignores the Sacred Books, and the centuries of Civilization of the people of India, treating them intellectually as South Sea Barbarians.

There was the same reason in both cases: Paul and the Modern Missionary were, with exceptions of very few, totally ignorant of the intellectual, spiritual, and moral, environment of the Religion, into which they were penetrating. God is no respecter of persons: he had not left the Greek race at the time of Paul without a clear conception of Right and Wrong, of sorrow following sin, knowledge of a Future State, and the great mystery of Holiness. No one can read the Immortal Survivals of Greek Learning without feeling that the Hellenic Σοφία was παιδαγωγός to Christ. And Augustine of Hippo, and his contemporaries, recognized Plato as a great ally.

Paul in his nescience ignored the Greek Schools of Philosophy: the New Testament did not exist in his time: so he depended entirely on such portions of the Old, as it seemed good to him to make use of.

If rightly handled by the Missionary the great principles of Morality, Holiness, and Faith in a superhuman Power, submission to a Divine leading, might be enforced by quotations from the Hindu Sages, Zoroaster, Confucius, and Buddha. The Missionary is tempted to consider the learning of past ages, anything beyond the Shibboleth of his Training College, and the orbit of his reading, to be the work of the Devil, and to condemn the great races of Ancient Days to unconditional Hell Fire.

Some young Hindu youths in the year 1893-4 acted the Play of "Sakóntala" in the English Translation from the original Sanskrit, and one of the actors remarked in a letter to the Translator dated May, 1893, as follows:

"Our object in acting Hindu Plays is to bring home to the "Hindu the good lessons, that our ancient authors are able to teach "us. If there is one lesson in these days more than another, which "forces itself on our minds, it is that our age is turning its back "on Creeds and Dogmas. We are hurrying forward to a Chaos, in "which all existing Religious Conceptions, and even the great "principles of Morality, may in the end be submerged, and as the "general tenour of Indian thought is to reject what is old, and "absorb all that is new, it becomes an urgent question, whether "a great Intellectual and Moral Revolution, which has no founda- "tion in the Past, can produce lasting benefits to the people." (Williams' "Sakóntala," 7th edition.)

The Brahmanical Religious Conception has lasted about three thousand years, among a population of two hundred millions: it may be about to expire, leaving no capacity in the intellects of the highly educated Hindu to admit the supernatural element as a factor in his spiritual inquiries. The last state will be worse than the first, and the Epoch of Theosophy, Mormonism, Comteism, Agnosticism, Unitarianism, and Theism, will have arrived.

Such may be the lot of the educated: as regards those who are totally devoid of Culture, I quote the following story:

I heard an open-air preacher describe the case of an old China woman, good, moral, devout, who daily on her rosary pronounced the name of Buddha: this was her way of Salvation. A young female Missionary tried to explain to her, that she should substitute the name of Jesus Christ for that of Buddha: she replied that she had found Buddha sufficient for 73 years, and could not change: she could no more have comprehended the reason suggested by the Missionary for taking Jesus Christ, than she could have explained to her the reason why she took Buddha. Such must be the intellectual position of Millions, passing through Life into Eternity.

III.

THE USELESS PROLONGATION OF THE LIFE OF A RELIGIOUS CONCEPTION BEYOND THE EPOCH, FOR WHICH IT WAS INTENDED.

A. Zoroastrian.
B. Hebrew.

In looking back in the History of Mankind we mark a Progress, or at least a change, in everything Human, the result of wider knowledge, greater experience, intellectual growth, and enlarged vision. The sports of children satisfy the child: a tribe of men is but the expression of the concentrated personality of each individual: he is not exactly like his grandfather, nor will his grandson be exactly like him. Any one of us, who has lived to know five generations of men, two older, one contemporary, and two younger, know this, and an old-fashioned person, who has lost step with his own generation, is usually deemed the survival of the least fit. So is it with every Human Branch of Knowledge. Ptolemy the Geographer would scarcely hold his own in the Royal Geographical Society, or the great Greek Astronomers at the Greenwich Observatory. So is it with the Conception of God, and the duty of Man: there are unhappy survivals, who have outlived their Epoch, and the great difficulty is to bring home to them in their semi-blind state a sense of their intellectual and spiritual position: any person, who still believed in the rotation of the Sun, would be a scientific phenomenon. In life we meet with old men and women, who try to hold their heads above their fellows, because they have known better days. So is it with the moribund Religious Conceptions of the Parsi or Zoroastrian, and the Hebrew, whose position as regards Past, Present, and Future I now pass under review with rigid impartiality. In the History of Man they are interesting Phenomena. How I should have enjoyed a conversation with a devout believer in Jupiter, Apollo, and Minerva, or a votary of Horus and Isis, and Amen Ra, or one who placed his implicit trust in Asher, the great God. I have had the opportunity of sweet converse with a Parsi Dastúr who believes in Ahriman, and exposes the lifeless corpse of his Parents and child to be torn and consumed by Vultures, and with a Hebrew, who still circumcises his males, and believes, that he is on a higher spiritual platform in his relation to God than the rest of mankind. It is an interesting, and not uninstructive, study, and an additional proof of the hopeless folly of mankind, when the mind is darkened by isolation and prejudice.

A. *Zoroastrian.*

About one hundred thousand most respectable subjects of the Empress of India, known as Parsi, resident in the Bombay Presidency, are all that survive of the Religion, which Zoroaster has the credit of having founded. They are wealthy, educated, and monogamists. Their Sacred Books in Zend, and Pahlavi, have been translated into English. Their Conception is purely Monotheistic, and there have never been temples, images, or altars. They reverence Fire, as the refulgent symbol of God, but it is not correct to call them worshippers of Fire. The assertion, that they admit a Dualism of two independent and hostile Spiritual Powers, is a mistake. Their idea of the Evil Spirit is identical with the Hebrew idea of Satan. They believe in the Immortality of the Soul, a Life to come, and Rewards and Punishment hereafter. Their Moral System is: "Good words, good thoughts, good deeds: think nothing but the Truth, speak nothing but the Truth, and do nothing but what is proper."

They unquestionably came into contact with the Hebrews at the time of the Hebrew Captivity in Babylon. Cyrus the King must have recognized a resemblance of the Religious Conception of the Hebrews, to the Persian, and to this may be attributed his wonderful kindness. As far as can be judged from pre-Exilic writings, the Hebrews had no knowledge of a life beyond the Grave until after their return from the Captivity; and even in the time of our Lord it was an open question, for on this subject the Pharisees and Sadducees differed. The name of Satan appears only three times in pre-Exilic Books: hence it is inferred, that the Hebrews borrowed these two Ideas from the Zoroastrians. It is noteworthy, that the Hebrews returned from Babylon uncompromising Monotheists: possibly contact with the Zorastrians led to this change also, for when the Hebrews went into Captivity they had fallen very low in their Idolatrous tendencies (Ezekiel, viii).

However 2,400 years have passed since then, and this great Religious Conception has shrunk into this insignificant survival. As a rule there were no Proselytes sought for or received: it is stated, that this policy has been lately suggested. No halo surrounds this remnant: they are hopeless exiles from their ancient country, have abandoned the Languages of their forefathers and adopted an Indian Vernacular; they still preserve a peculiar headdress. They have given birth to no new Religious Conception. For what possible advantage to the Human race do they survive?

B. *Hebrew.*

The Hebrew is scattered in every Christian and Mahometan country, but rarely beyond. They have abandoned their ancestral dress, and not only lost their own ancient Language, but speak twenty or thirty mutually unintelligible forms of speech; still, they possess their Sacred Books in the original Hebrew and Aramaic. Among their number in this century are some of the most illustrious Scholars, and wealthiest Merchants. It is necessary to describe them in fuller detail:

(1) Exordium.
(2) Population, Country, Language, party divisions, absence of race, or Nationality; the only link a Religious Conception.
(3) Legal customs: circumcision, food. Ritual: absence of all Spirituality.
(4) Sacred Books, modern Creed; desire to return to Palestine, and recommence Sacrifice of Animals.
(5) Assertion that all Virtue and Morals come from them, and that God only cares for them, while no exertions have ever been made by them to propagate their Religious views to their fellow-creatures.
(6) Idolatry having ceased, their *raison d'être* has disappeared; cruel treatment in the Middle Ages, entire Liberty now.
(7) Conclusion.

The Hebrew Diasporà is but a drop in the Ocean, when the population of the World is considered, nor is it by many centuries the most ancient. As regards Human Science and Art, the Hebrews contributed nothing to the common stock of Human Knowledge: as regards Divine things, they contributed a Library of Books in two Languages, the Hebrew and the Aramaic, the earliest of which could not have been committed to writing in an obsolete form of the Phœnician Script before 800 B.C., and the latest, the Wisdom of Sirach, about the Christian era. The Christian Religious Conception came into existence at the time of the destruction of the Hebrew Nationality, confessedly from Hebrew sources.

The Hebrew race has maintained its own Religious Conception to this day, but in a mutilated form, having lost its essential features and its local base.

Volumes have been written on this subject, but rarely, if ever, has it been treated impartially: partizans on both sides have embittered; enthusiasts have obscured. I desire to accept facts, as admitted by both parties, and discuss philosophically the problem of the cause of the prolongation of a Conception and Ritual suitable to the Nineteenth century B.C. into so different and unsympathetic an Epoch as the Nineteenth century A.D., and the attempt to maintain Institutions, originally adapted to a semi-barbarous tribe of released slaves in a very low round of the ladder of Culture, by a community transplanted far from their original homes and scattered in small companies in many and distant lands. Let us reflect on the gross ignorance of Solomon, or his exaggeration, when addressing God (II Chronicles, i, 9): "Now, O Lord God . . . Thou hast made me king over a people like the dust of the Earth in multitude." At the outside there could have been but four Millions, if so many: the area would not have supported more, and there was no Diasporà then.

Some write, as if the existing Hebrew population amounted to twelve Millions, but a more careful study reduces it to ten Millions, scattered in every country ruled by Christian or Mahometan Governments, China being the only exception. From the point of view of the Ethnologist the Hebrew has ceased to be a Nation, as the scattered fragments have become portions of at least twenty Nations; and it is doubtful, whether they are a "race" in the Endogamist sense, of which the Hindu is a specimen, where there is no admixture of foreign blood by marriage out of the particular Caste. From the time of the twelve sons of Jacob marrying alien wives down to the present date there has been a constant accretion of Gentile wives, Gentile slaves purchased, and incorporated, Proselytes of the Gate, and the absorption of smaller tribes like the Gibeonites and the Kenites, and the Idumeans, who were forcibly circumcised. So we are dealing, in fact, with the holders of a peculiar Religious Conception, and the believers in certain Sacred Books, and nothing more. "Abraham's seed" is thus by a figure of speech converted into a great multitude. We can scarcely for one moment suppose that the Jews of Abyssinia, India, and China, are descended after the flesh from Abraham.

And this great Diasporà is rent into divers sections, differing very considerably from each other, the rift being much greater than the one, which separates the Roman Catholic from the Protestant or Greek Churches. In no one case are they in enjoyment of political independence : they are as strangers in different countries, and speak totally different Languages. If the word race or tribe be applied to them, it is only as a phrase: their only real link is their historical Religious Belief.

The modern Hebrews are divided among themselves into categories:

> I. The Talmudist or Conservative, who differ little in kind, though in degree, from the Pharisee of the time of our Lord: they give tithe of anise and cumin, and have not the least perception of the nature of true Worship or true Religion, not for the Jews only, but for all Mankind. Among them are many holy individuals blameless according to the Law, and waiting, like old Simeon, for the consolation of Israel : clearly such persons, whether

German, English, or Russian, are anachronisms in the Nineteenth century.

II. Next to them come the Chasídim, founded by a Rabbi in the Eighteenth century: they turn from the Talmud to the Kabála mysticism: they go in for asceticism, purity, holiness, rather than Knowledge: they feel that the Holy Spirit operates through certain chosen men of their number, Zadíkin, and who are in a humble sense mediators between God and His believing people. They make pilgrimages to visit such holy men, and seek their blessing: they interpret Scriptures, not according to the letter, but the Spirit: a vast mass of Literature has sprung up around them: as Swedenborgianism is to Christianity, so are their tenets to the ordinary Belief and Practice.

III. Reformed, Advanced, Liberal. Moses Mendelssohn (b. 1729) was the founder. This division ranges from those, who only reject the Traditions of the Rabbi, to those who threw overboard the Old Testament, and are rationalists.

IV. Those who are neither renegades nor agnostics, but are intellectually estranged from orthodoxy, and yet unassociated with any Reform movement within the fold: they are critics towards every School of thought presented to them, and yet stand outside those Schools.

V. The nominal Hebrews, occupied with things of this world, with no sense of Religion in them.

VI. The Karaite of the Krimea, few in number. They have never accepted the Talmud, and hold to Moses and the Prophets alone: their name means "written," because they keep to the written Law, and reject the oral Law of Tradition; in fact, as regards Talmudic Judaism, they are Protestants.

There are signs of a movement; the slumber of centuries has been disturbed. The young and educated Hebrews have become convinced, that they have outgrown the Rabbinical Laws of the last generation: they have a lofty ideal in striving to promote a Spiritual Life in a moribund Community: they wish to simplify their Ritual, and remove formal Prayers, no longer in consonance with modern ideas. It is in struggles of this kind, that passionate aspirations are generated, and new Epochs created. It is by such means, that Nature gives birth to new forms, and the Human Intellect develops new possibilities.

The modern Jew fondly believes, that the Law, as the mediating link between God and Man, fulfils something of the same office as the person of Christ in the various phases of Christianity: but is it so? Is it possible, that ceremonial observances, particular meats, washing of cups and platters, can hold the same influence over the mind of the Nineteenth century as they did in elder days? for the Person of Christ remains an everlasting ideal from generation to generation; yesterday, to-day, and for ever.

Deep-seated particularism, puerility of large portions of their Law, egotistic self-righteousness, unrighteous contempt, and heedlessness for the Souls of contemporary Millions, are the features of their Religious life. The very absence of all social persecution, their admission to all the privileges of Gentiles, must undo them. They feel, that their armour of defence or offence is not suited for the present form of battle; that it is a husk, of which the kernel is gone, the stock of a tree of which the branches have been cut off. Development is the very lifeblood of Religion: it is part of the great burgeoning, the great harvest, of the Soul and intellect of each generation. The Jewish Synagogue represents a glass receptacle for Gas, but the supply of Gas has been cut off, and there is no Light.

If a Religion feels, that its very existence depends upon its Morality, how can it tolerate the existence side by side of two such precepts, as

"Thou shalt not wear a garment of mixed stuff of divers sort,"
and
"Thou shalt love thy neighbour as thyself."

It is only now that the amazing *idealization* of the Law is breaking down, when it is forcing itself upon the minds capable of valuing historic Proof, that the Pentateuch must be weighed in the balance of actual *historic* worth, and, subjected to the scalpel of Criticism, robbed of its supernatural glamour, that the modern Hebrew feels the want of a dominant and consistent Doctrine, adequate and comprehensive, Soul-satisfying and rational, which can set forth in its entire compass the relation of the Individual to Society and to God.

It seems, as if it were impossible for the Hebrew to burst the bonds of Legalism and Particularism, and remain a Hebrew still. The great World has been revealed, and the great Nations have passed, and are passing over, the stage of Humanity; and it seems ridiculous for a petty tribe of a few Millions, a tribe broken up into fragments, on different levels of Civilization and speaking different Languages, to claim to be the special people of the Almighty. Such a claim may have been intelligible centuries before Christ, but is no longer so at this Epoch: the very fact, that it lays stress on the mutilation of the body of males, indicates how far behind it has been left in the Religious development of worshipping a God, who is a Spirit. How can a Religion, which does not put itself forward as Universal, and which does not make efforts to propagate itself, hope to maintain its existence in an Epoch of progress, and World-embracing enlightenment?

Three attempts were made to reduce the oral Law to system and order in writing: the last succeeded. Rabbi Jehudah, 200 A.D., completed the work after immense exertion, but as soon as it was completed it was obsolete in many parts by the lapse of time, and change of environment. The Temple was gone; Rome had cut short the jurisdiction of the Sanhedrin; Palestine and its Agrarian Laws had disappeared: however, the Code was kept, to be in use in the dim and remote period of the Restoration of Israel.

But, as stated above, the written Mishnah became the subject of development and discussion: new Traditions sprang up, new methods were invented, and the Gemára ensued in a twofold form, for the Jews were hopelessly scattered:

(1) Redacted at Tiberias about 390 A.D., expressing the view of the Palestine Schools, and written in the Eastern Aramaic Language.
(2) At Syra in Babylonia, 365–427 A.D., which was finally closed at the end of the Fifth century. This is written in the Language of Western Aramaic.

They have not come down to us perfect: the Babylonian Talmud (for so the two parts were called) is four times as large as the so-called Jerusalem Talmud. During the persecution of the Jews by the Persians, the Schools were closed for eighty years: all further development was stopped, and the Talmud, thus built up, obtained supreme authority.

The Mishnah is in as pure Hebrew as can be expected in those days: the people spoke a corrupt Aramaic, mixed with Greek and Latin loan-words: the Mishnah itself could not exclude such terms. The Gemára was in Aramaic, the Language of the common people.

The Talmud may be said to embody the Civil and Canonical Law; it comprises, in addition, Philosophy, Medicine, History, Jurisprudence, and practical duty; it is a supplement to the Pentateuch, and it took 1,000 years of Natural life to produce it, from the return from exile to the end of the Fifth century A.D. (Deutch.)

Let us think out the rite of Circumcision. Nothing can more fully illustrate the unfitness of the Hebrew Ritual and Religion for the present Epoch: it is indecent, unseemly, carnal, by the necessity of Nature restricted to one sex, a survival of the practices of savage races, such as caste-marks, mutilation of the body, extraction of teeth; it is even akin to castration. In the newspapers of the Jews we read of Circumcision by chloroform, and appointments to be made: let us think of the relations gathered together in some place of Worship, to attend the initiation of a child, as in the time of Moses and Zipporah (Exodus, iv, 25); it is a bloody operation: in the case of an adult proselyte it can scarcely be conceived, that an inquirer would submit to it. The Hebrew Prophets in their time suggested a circumcision of the foreskin of the heart. We read of the ceremony taking place surrounded with ceremonial in Mahometan Courts; of the Sultan paying the expense of the circumcision of the son of one of his Ministers by way of compliment. In the Memoirs of Gordon of Khartúm, we read how he circumcised two boys: we can only trust that they were Heathen, and not Christian, boys. The rite of circumcision is practised by the lowest and most barbarous African tribes, and the naked statues of the early Egyptian Dynasties reveal unmistakably, that the men of those remote days were circumcised, but not as a Religious rite. Only imagine a new Religion being started, of which the symbol should be the cutting off of the thumb-nail, which at least would be decent, manifest to the outer world, and apply to both sexes, and the followers of this new craze being so infatuated as to use as a term of reproach the words, "uncut thumb-nail"! and yet we read that the Hebrews twitted the tribes in their neighbourhood as "uncircumcised," because they had not adopted this indecent and barbarous practice, and in many cases they forcibly imposed the rite upon tribes defeated in battle. (Josephus, Book xiii, cap. 9.)

The idea of atonement for sins by the slaughter of cattle, or birds, is a frightful anachronism, and practically among the Hebrews has ceased to exist Centuries ago, their Prophets told them, that the sacrifice of God was a contrite heart, yet the Hebrew in his Synagogue still prays for the restoration of bloody Sacrifice: it was the common feature of all the older Religions, but the wheels of the chariot of Civilization passed over it.

The idea of particular food comes next: why should particular classes of the Animal-Creation be called unclean, and unfit for Human consumption? in what way are swine, bred in European farms, more unclean than the sheep, or the ox? Is not this prejudice of the Hebrew against swine something analogous to the prejudice of the Gentile against the Hebrew? What right have we to call anything common or unclean?

I quote an extract from a Hebrew Periodical: "Do our Institu-
" tions show such an attachment? For weeks already, the
" unleavened cakes required for consumption on the approaching
" Easter, have already been in preparation, to supply the 70,000
" Jews residing in London, and also those in the Provinces and in
" the Colonies. But it is from Holland or Germany, that those
" must get the Matzoth or Paschal cakes, who are anxious to have
" them done according to strict legal requirement. And yet the
" Matzoth-bakeries are under the supervision of the Chief Rabbi
" and his assessor. The shortcomings in the preparation of the

"Matzoth are an open secret. The Chief Rabbi knows them, the assessor knows them, and every (oral) law-abiding Hebrew knows them. Do we not give the lie to the Memorial, where it says that we cling with all devotion to our ancient faith? or does it refer to our brethren in Russia, and not to us? The Gentile reader will have much difficulty in comprehending the point of the impeachment."

The penalty for eating leavened bread is exclusion from the community of Israel: "That Law has been universally accepted as divine, and necessarily so; for, if the Law of Moses is still binding, it cannot possibly provide for all the contingencies, that must arise in the course of centuries, and under conditions radically different from those under which it was given. Any neglect, therefore, of its provisions, is an act of rebellion against the God of Israel; and if persevered in, must lead to the total refutation of Judaism, and that is what it is actually and rapidly coming to."

When I visit, as a Magistrate, the prisons in the neighbourhood of London at Easter-time, I find long sticks of unleavened bread, sent in by some pious Hebrew for the food of his brethren, who are paying the penalty of their crimes, very often crafty, unrepenting, villains.

Then comes the Law with regard to slaughtering animals. No uneducated Hindu can be more ridiculous than a Hebrew, residing in London, and boasting of the spirituality of his Religious Belief. "'Shechita' is the method of slaughtering animals. The Law prohibits the eating of blood. Every precaution, therefore, has to be taken in the killing of Jewish meat to draw off the *maximum* of blood from the body. First, the animal's hind-feet are bound together; then, by means of a pulley-arrangement the animal is 'cast' upon its back. The left fore-foot is now secured to prevent its rising from the ground, and in this recumbent position its throat is cut by a broad long knife, which has been previously sharpened to perfection. The trachea, jugular veins, and carotid arteries, are completely severed, so that the system is effectually drained of blood. A special training is required for those, who practise as slaughterers, a feature of which is to learn to sharpen the knife skilfully and detect the slightest notch on the blade. 'Shechita' has the further advantage of being most humane. It is practically painless. The severance of the windpipe by a faultlessly sharp instrument has the effect of depriving the animal of sensibility in somewhat less than a minute. The movements it continues to make for some time afterwards are purely reflex. Poleaxing, on the other hand, or strangulation, is a longer and less refined process, besides that its stunning effect is less certain in the case of a tough and vigorous animal."

No Buddhist or Jain community can exceed the Hebrew in the precautions taken lest, that which entereth the man should defile the man: this indicates how low in the scale of Religious Beliefs the Hebrew has fallen.

"KOSHER-MEAT.—The Hebrews of Birmingham, not satisfied
"with the present 'Kosher' meat-supply, want to establish a
"co-operative association of their own. Every week between
"5,000 and 6,000 lbs. of 'Kosher'-meat are consumed in Birmingham,
"and about 300 head of 'Kosher'-poultry. In order that the
"requirements of the Jewish faith in respect to the method of
"killing and the freedom from blemish of the animal may be faith-
"fully observed, an officer, called Shochet, is appointed, whose
"duty it is to see to these matters. Before he is qualified for the
"office he has to undergo a severe examination, and the appoint-
"ment carries with it a good salary. When he has placed his
"seal upon a joint, there can be no question that it is sound
"and wholesome meat. This circumstance explains why many
"Christians buy 'Kosher'-meat. In a neighbouring town, about
"one-eighth the size of Birmingham, there are about a dozen
"Hebrews, but they are obliged to have their Shochet, who
"receives a salary of 25s. per week, and their regular 'Kosher'
"butcher. Sometime ago the congregation made a change in their
"butcher, and with the transfer of the Jewish custom went a not
"inconsiderable portion of the Gentile trade, showing the Christian
"appreciation of 'Kosher'-meat. The 15th of this month is the
"New Year's Day of the Hebrew calendar, and just prior to that
"occasion, as is the case at our festive season, there is a very brisk
"trade in the 'Kosher'-poultry and meat-shops."

Men of the ancient days were more than ready to refer extraordinary appearances, marvellous discoveries, sublime teaching, and
writings on metal, clay, skins, or papyrus, to the direct intervention
of the Deity. Gross ignorance prevailed, and everything was
swallowed; but, when variations in the Text of the writings came
into existence, each party tried to support their own Text by
anathemas, and violence, and this delusion prevails to the present
day. The orthodox Hebrew will pin his faith to one particular
Text, and rejects all argument. In 1851, at Nablus, a Samaritan
Rabbi produced a copy of the Torah on parchment for inspection,
and assured Mr. Finn, the Consul at Jerusalem, and myself, that it
was written by the pen of a son of Aaron: he had no difficulty in
believing such a monstrous assertion.

I quote the following remarks, made by a speaker at an Islington
Conference, 1892 :—
"Scepticism, which is such a marked feature of our time, is
"making inroads upon the ancient faith: old Rabbinic customs
"are being discarded; the yearly festivals, the Tfillin and the
"Tsith, are no longer observed with the same scrupulous care.
"It has been proposed more than once to transfer the Sabbath-
"Worship to Sunday, that thus an additional day might be secured

"for the pressing requirements of secular life. Recent criticism
"upon the Old Testament has made a deep impression. There is
"a prevalent drifting from the old landmarks. Many feel, that the
"Mosaic ritual is an impossibility, and that the hopes concerning
"the Messiah have proved a failure; and some are wildly asking,
"'Have we any Future?' Or does it not seem, as if it had served
"its purpose, and was no longer applicable to the requirements of
"modern life? Rationalism is eating its way into the very heart.
"But this disintegration must sooner or later be followed by recon-
"struction; for the Hebrew, with his history and traditional
"associations, cannot live without God, and so many are being led
"in their weary search for the God, whom their forefathers knew,
"to embrace Christianity, or some form of Unitarianism.

"But it may be said, that these sceptical influences are only felt
"by a certain section. This is in part true, but it is also true, that
"even amongst the so-called orthodox there is a spirit of restless
"dissatisfaction. Many feel, that the hopes of the Old Testament
"have resulted in failure, and the drift towards Christianity is very
"marked. They imitate Christian methods, come to services and
"sermons in our churches, read the New Testament, and recognize
"the noble qualities in the life of Jesus of Nazareth; and when
"the revised translation of the New Testament appeared, they
"spoke of it in the highest terms as a book, of which the race
"might be justly proud. M. Debré, Rabbi of Neuilly, near Paris,
"writes in the *Jewish Quarterly*, that now newborn children are
"brought to the synagogue to receive the blessing of the Rabbi,
"just as Christian children are brought to Baptism. There is also
"a ceremony of initiation for boys and girls of twelve and thirteen
"years, at which the boys appear in black and the girls in white,
"very much like Confirmation, and for which they are carefully
"prepared by the Rabbi. The Rabbi is now summoned to the
"bedside of the sick and dying; the coffin is strewn with flowers
"as amongst Christians; the Hebrew prayers are replaced by others
"in the vernacular; the organ and choir have found a place in the
"synagogue; sermons are frequent; and an afternoon service is
"provided for the ladies; the Rabbi dresses very much as the
"ordinary clergyman."

It is necessary to state what the Hebrew does believe.

Maimonides laid down the following thirteen articles as constituting the Creed:

1. The belief in the existence of a Creator.
2. ,,   ,,   His Unity.
3. ,,   ,,   His Incorporeality.
4. ,,   ,,   His eternity.
5. All Worship due to Him *alone*.

6. The belief in Prophecy.
7. „ „ that Moses was the greatest of all Prophets, both before and after Him.
8. „ „ that Torah was revealed to Moses on Mount Sinai.
9. „ „ in the Immutability of the revealed Torah.
10. „ „ that God knows the actions of men.
11. „ „ in Reward and Punishment.
12. „ „ in the coming of the Messiah.
13. „ „ in the Resurrection of the Dead.

(Schechter, "Studies in Judaism," p. 199.)

The *Messenger* describes thus what it is to be a Hebrew:

It is to be in sympathy with whatever is pure and ennobling.
It is to translate into life the golden texts of our sages.
It is to be faithful to the Hebrew ideals, which indicate the loftiest Humanity.
It is to hold fast to the essentials and to breathe into form and ceremony all the spirituality and beauty we can.
It is to lead a modest life, to avoid extravagance and exaggeration, to be prudent, economical, and thrifty.
It is to cultivate the home-virtues, to sanctify the dwelling by home-Worship, to promote kindness and charity.
It is to join in any movement for Human betterment, to avoid dissension and bitterness, to cherish the brightest ambitious, and do our utmost to swell the choir of Human adoration of the One Only God.

The Doctrines of the Resurrection of the Dead, a Judgment-Day, Rewards and Punishments, Life Everlasting, require separate notice. Had the Hebrew before the Captivity in Babylon any knowledge of these Doctrines? The argument of the Book of Job seems to indicate, that the idea was unknown to the writer of that Book. However, Moses, who is credited with a knowledge of all the wisdom of the Egyptians, must have known of that important feature of the Egyptian Religious Conception, and yet he is silent on the subject, and makes no use of this potent lever to secure the obedience of his hearers. Even to this day, the prospect, or threat, of Hell Fire hereafter, is the only argument, which tells on the drunken and profligate Christian. The Sheol of the Hebrew does not represent the idea. In 1 Samuel, xxviii, 19, we read that good and bad all go to the same place. Contact with the Zoroastrians at Babylon must have given the Hebrew the first idea: the Hebrew Diasporà at Alexandria must have heard of the Immortality of the Soul, as distinct from a Body reduced to ashes, in the writing of Plato, and it is obvious, that in the centuries preceding the great Anno Domini, the idea was current, though an open question: it represents a great development of Hebrew thought since the time of Moses.

Claude Montefiore, in the *Jewish Quarterly Review*, 1892, writes on the effect of Biblical Criticism upon the Hebrew Religion:

"Far more emphasis is laid on Hebrew rites than on Hebrew
"dogma: the practical execution of the written and oral Law is
"the essential characteristic: some are ready to give up all the
"dogma, if they may retain the rites and ceremonies, retain
"them, emptied of all Religious value, bereft of all Religious
"life. Theoretical heterodoxy is thus united with practical
"orthodoxy."

Then, again, I quote the following:

"There is one narrow dogma, which, because it is not touched
"by criticism or philosophy, it is open for the "Unitarian" to add
"to his total store. That dogma is the Mission of Israel, and that
"dogma we still retain. We do believe, that the Divine Ruler and
"Educator of mankind chose out the Nation of Israel for a peculiar
"religious task, and we do believe, that even now, when the Nation
"has been changed into a Community, that task is not concluded.
"Between Agnosticism upon the one hand, and Trinitarianism
"upon the other, the Hebrew steers a middle course. His Theism is
"opposed alike to a wonder-working superstition, and to a soulless
"Deism. Who can say that a historical faith of such a nature may
"not even exercise a certain influence for good by the very fact of
"its existence? And as it becomes more and more sensible of the
"unique position, which it might claim among the Religions of the
"civilized World, who can say that that silent influence may not
"gradually be exchanged for direct teaching and admonition? So
"believing, may we not still regard ourselves as Hebrew, though
"we disbelieve in miracles, deny the unity and Mosaic authorship of
"the Pentateuch, and *consequently* do certainly not observe 'the
"inherited law in *all* its details'?"

The idea of Restoration to Palestine, and of Sacrifice in a new Temple on Mount Moriah, is visionary, carnal, and unpractical. The Hebrew community of the Nineteenth century includes the enlightened statesman, the profound philosopher, the gifted Scholar, the eloquent Christianized ordained convert, as well as the degraded keeper of low inns and brothels, and the scavenger class in South Russia: they speak different Languages, are on different rounds of Human Culture, with no sentiments in common, but the repute of being descendants of Abraham nearly 4,000 years ago, which again is very doubtful, as an ethnological fact, and quite incapable of proof. Their numbers, even in the lowest quotation of seven

Millions, far exceed the limited resources of the petty Province of Palestine.

In the office of the Royal Geographical Society, I have had the area of the Promised Land, exclusive of the Dead Sea, and Sea of Galilee, scientifically measured, and the area amounts to twelve thousand square miles, slightly in excess of the area of Belgium: but there is this difference: the area of Belgium is nearly entirely culturable, that of the Promised Land is chiefly mountainous and unculturable, as I know by experience in two tours at long intervals, with all the experience of an Anglo-Indian Land-Revenue official. The population of Belgium is six Millions, and it has the largest population to the square mile in Europe. The Promised Land will hardly support a population of Four Millions.

Must a fresh slaughter of women and children and peaceful inhabitants accompany the second Hebrew Invasion? We have only to imagine the Maori trying to play this game on a small scale in New Zealand, or the Hindu on a large scale in India. They might proclaim, and with truth, that their ancestors possessed the land, and assert that the Creator gave it to them for "*an everlasting possession,*" and, as it is a matter of pure sentiment, if they were strong enough, it would be difficult to disprove.

It is time to take the Hebrew down from the pedestal, on which mediaeval ignorance has placed him, and to assure him, that he belongs to one of the ordinary races of mankind, by no means the first in the classification of Human greatness, and that he must behave as such.

In the *Jewish Quarterly Review* for January, 1893, appears an article by a Mr. Oswald John Simon on "Authority and Dogma." The Synagogues are constituted under a certain Act of Parliament, 1870, and the Chief Rabbi of the United Congregations of the British Empire lately inhibited a minister for the following reasons:

(1) His objection "to offer prayer for the restoration of the sacrificial rite."
(2) His published utterance contains matter, which is surmised to be at variance with tradition.

Mr. Simon's strictures apply to the first reason: he remarks, that belief in the restoration of sacrifices has never been held in the present generation to be an essential article of his creed. It has no place in the Thirteen Articles, which are found in the orthodox Prayer-book. The rite of sacrifice is one, which is characteristic of an age not only bygone, but necessarily incapable of living over again by reason of the ordinary law of cause and effect. The ancient rite of shedding the blood of cattle (shared with all the heathen world) was nothing but a means to an end, and essentially of a temporary character. The Human mind is incapable of reverting in the long order of progress: if it were true, that a peculiar "ism" or system is stationary, Human character is not, nor is it possible to stop the growth and the change of ideal in the long march of countless generations: a social or religious practice, after having been obsolete for nearly two thousand years, cannot re-establish itself. Prayer has been substituted for slaying of cattle. Even if it were possible, that they were restored to Canaan, it is not conceivable, that their return would take place without the advantages of Science; there might be again a gorgeous temple, but it would be fitted with electric light. Ancient Judea would not be restored without railways and a printing-press; the culture of the age, and the environment, would accompany the returning Hebrew; there would necessarily be a library of literature of the World in Jerusalem, but there would be no butcher's *abattoir* for killing calves and lambs. This line of argument applies equally to the Sacerdotalism of modern Christianity. Religion can never mean stagnation, but development. The attempt to limit the progress of Religious thought is futile; to choke Religion by the practice of the Middle Ages or the early centuries of Christianity, seems analogous to praying for the restoration of Temple Sacrifice.

Dr. Herzl, in his Pamphlet on a Hebrew State, argues as follows: that the Hebrew cannot assimilate with other nations: so much the worse for the Hebrew, as well as the Gypsy; in that case he must retire into a corner.

"We are one People. We have honestly striven everywhere to "merge ourselves in the social life of surrounding communities, "and to preserve only the faith of our fathers. It has not been "permitted to us. In vain are we loyal patriots, in some places "our loyalty running to extremes; in vain do we make the same "sacrifices of life and property as our fellow-citizens; in vain do "we strive to increase the fame of our native land in Science and "Art, or her wealth by trade and commerce. In countries, where "we have lived for centuries, we are still cried down as strangers; "and often by those, whose ancestors were not yet domiciled in the "land, where Jews had already made experience of suffering. Yet, "in spite of all, we are loyal subjects, loyal as the Huguenots, "who were forced to emigrate. Oh that we could only be left "in peace!"

He then asks for a portion of the Globe large enough for the requirements of his so-called Nation, which has ceased to be so for 1,800 years.

It goes without saying, that Hebrew emigrants have as much right to as large an area of other people's land as they can lay their hands on. Nothing prevents a Hebrew Company, under men such as Barnáto, annexing another Ma-Shónaland, slaughtering the indigenous inhabitants, and founding a new Palestine by the same unscrupulous methods, which Joshua used at the time of the Exodus. What is insisted upon is, that this has nothing to do with Religion, or the benefit of the Human race, Present or Future. The Hebrew cannot at this Epoch be deemed to have a Mission to civilize alien races, and bring the souls of the Heathen to God, which is the only Mission worthy of notice. They might have done so in the centuries preceding the great Anno Domini : Jonah set them an example; their Prophets pointed out this Duty; they were ahead of the races of mankind at that period in their Conception of the Divine: it was possible to do so in Asia, as in 550 B.C. Buddha had preached a Universal Gospel of Altruism as opposed to Hebrew Egoism; and in the great Anno Domini a Light to lighten the Gentiles, and a Power to turn the World upside down, came unmistakably from one born of a Hebrew Mother in a city of the tribe of Benjamin. But they lost their opportunity: they forfeited the great title of the "Chosen People," and assumed the situation of the "Rejected People," as they had forfeited all claim to God's Promises, and come, in spite of knowledge, under all the penalties detailed in Deuteronomy upon disobedient children.

Even supposing, that by a marvellous stroke of Fortune, the French Nation were willing to surrender their claim to Syria, inclusive of the Holy Land, in the event of the much desired disappearance of the "Unspeakable Turk": is there in the Hebrew race a power to constitute an administration of the country? Imagine a Senate consisting of a Rothschild, Baron Herz, and some of the leading Hebrew politicians of each of the European Nations: add to these representatives of the great Hebrew Scholars, and men of Science, totally unversed in political affairs: add to these Hebrews from Hounsditch and from the back streets of Paris and Vienna, Karaites from the Krimea, keepers of brothels and gambling-houses, from South Russia, and the veriest scum of Poland. It is possible, that in the lowest ranks of this heterogeneous mass some one might assert, that he was of the lineage of David, and claim to be the King of this Restored Nation. A new Temple would have to be erected, and the Mosque of Omar destroyed, which would rouse the Mahometan World to fury. The Butcher's Shop of Sacrifice of Animals would have to be reopened, and pigeons and turtle-doves have their throats cut; while the male infants were having their bodies operated on under chloroform to prevent cries of anguish. It is of no use talking in a pious, romantic, sensational, goody-goody way of the restoration of the Hebrews to the Holy Land without remembering the possibility of all the incidents of extermination of the present Gentile inhabitants, with which it must be accompanied.

More than one author has attempted to elaborate a Philosophy of Hebrew History, and no doubt there is ample room for reflection whether:

(1) The Hebrew race were ever on a different platform from the rest of the races of mankind, as they even to this day pretend to be.
(2) Whether they were intellectually, spiritually, worthy of the position, to which European Theologians have raised them. Asiatic Nations such as the Persian, Indian, Chinese, Japanese, would of course totally refuse to place them except in the lowest class of tribes.
(3) Whether their entire failure in the time of the Judges, the Kings, and their Sacerdotal Rule, to fulfil the most elementary principles of the Law, which they vaunted themselves about, does not lead to the impression, that the so-called Hebrew Dispensation was an entire failure, and not from God, *for God's plans can never fail.* It was not only, that they went after false gods in spite of their Law, their Priests and Prophets, but they failed grossly in Moral Character from the time of Hosea to the Captivity, as evidenced in Jeremiah, v, 7, 8.

Is not Islam the true representative in modern days of the old Hebrew of the Palestinian period? the same proud self-righteousness, the formal repetition of prayers in an unknown Language, the genuflexions as of a drilled regiment, the denial of any need of a Mediator, as the poor sinful man so many times a day bandies words with his Creator with no consciousness of sin. The murderer, the robber, the adulterer, repeat the formal Prayer with the same complacency as the Godfearing, holy worshipper, whose daily thoughts, words, and acts, are offerings on the altar. Then comes the degraded rite of circumcision, and the tolerated Polygamy and Divorce. The Mahometan Faith stands so far a step higher than the Hebrew as it is universal, not confined to the so-called sons of Abraham, though the physical differences of the Sephardim and Ezkanázim show that a common ancestry is problematical. Both call their Sacred Books "Kalam Illah," the Word of God; both, when they have a chance, are frightfully intolerant, one in persecuting professors of other Faiths, the other in resisting any secession from its own; both are unworthy of the Nineteenth century in the essential feature of a Religious Conception, *Spirituality.*

It can be remarked in ordinary life that, if anyone clings to an idea whether of his own importance, or his talents, or his lineage, it at last assumes to him the aspect of Truth: so is it with the Hebrew race: it really was a most unimportant one, during the time that it existed as a Nation, and filled a ridiculously small part in Ancient History: yet they have managed to get up a kind of glamour, composed partly of their discreditable Past, and partly of the prospect of a dim and remote Future, never likely to come, the nature of which is not spiritual, but grossly carnal and material, a return to the chief city of a petty little Province, which they entered 3,000 years ago by violence, and from which they were expelled by violence, as if the Worship of the Great Creator, or His precious Promises, or his Ubiquitous Presence in every part of His Great Creation, were localized in one petty Island, or one insignificant Region.

Israel, during the last two centuries, used to be in History a single mountain peak; all around was darkness; the mist has now cleared away, and we see a great range of Nations, and Israel assumes its proper insignificant proportion: it was a mere pawn in the great political game of Egypt and Assyria. It pleased the early Christian centuries to surround the Hebrew History with a halo: the contemporary Nations recognized no special merit; they knew the country and the people as a very common clay to tread upon.

We know, that it was very like every other Nation of its Epoch, and environment, like them in its lawful Worship and its Worship of strange deities, in its successes, in its unjustifiable attacks upon its neighbours, and in its defects: it had ordinary contact with other Nations, and ordinary commercial relations, and employed Tyrian idolaters of the grossest type to build the Temple: it joined in leagues and conspiracies against other tribes, and whatever it thought of itself, it was not thought of by its neighbours as a holy tribe. I quote the following from a Hebrew periodical in the United States: *The Peculiar People*, vol. vi, No. 3, p. 67:

" Devout Jews protest against the audacity of Gentiles in their
" attempt to convert them, as in the field of Religion they were the
" Masters, the witnesses of God, and the World sat at their feet.
" Let benevolent people turn to the Heathen, if they want to have
" converts. For the Jew to renounce Monotheism, a belief in one
" sole God, and accept a Triune God, is a step backwards; it is the
" last surviving remnant of Paganism."

Let us consider the Heavens and the Earth as a wonderful exhibition of Divine Wisdom, unchanged and unchangeable from the day of Creation; the return of Day and Night, the Revolution of the Seasons, the alternation of Life and Death, and the lessons, which they teach, and the gradual attainment of Knowledge by the children of Men. Can we suppose that the great Controller of the World would have condescended to teach one petty Semitic family, one unworthy tribe, amidst the Millions of His children, the details of ceremonial washing, and the mode of slaughtering beasts, while He failed to teach them, that the Sun did not revolve round the

Earth, and that their life in this World was as nothing compared to the Everlasting Life hereafter? If such petty Laws as the consulting of Ephods, the mutilation of the body, and empty ceremonial, were from the Lord, would they not have been universal to the Human race, and immutable, like the Laws, which regulate the rotation of the Globe? Does not the surface of that great Globe belong to Him? Can it be credited that he has a prejudice in favour of Banáras, or Mekka, or Jerusalem? Is not the History of Mankind one of stately Progress from Savagery to Barbarism, from Barbarism to Civilization, as Men advance from Childhood to the Adult Stage, and thence on to Fulness of Knowledge, and the reception of the greater Gifts of the most High?

The Hebrew of Palestine, as recorded in his own Sacred Books (for no other History alludes to him), was a hopeless creature, devoid of all idea of Philosophy, History, or Reason. According to him, like the Plymouth Brothers of modern days, he alone was to be saved: his Egotism appears at every page of his Annals: the Almighty cared for him *alone*: he was to judge and rule the World: he alone realized what God was, and what Morality was: all the rest of the world was unclean, ignorant, enemies of God, and *hated by God*. Some of the Protestants of the Middle Class at this day consign in the same way all, who do not look eye to eye, and thought to thought, with them on matters spiritual, to the uncovenanted mercies of Satan and Hell. But the Colony of Hebrews settled at Alexandria started a temple of their own at Leontopolis, and adopted the Greek Language and Customs. To their astonishment they found that Plato and Aristotle, by unassisted Reason, and that Holy Spirit, which comes from God to all pure and devout natures, had arrived at very much the same platform of thought as the Hebrew, but with an infinitely wider horizon, and supported their views by Λόγος, "Reason," mistranslated "Word," for Word is only the vehicle of Reason. Philo caught up the echo of Plato's sayings, and thence it found its way to the Gospel of John.

Nothing more marks the progress of the Human Intellect, and the expansion of Divine Government, than the Hebrew and Christian Dispensation, regarded solely from the Human standpoint. Nineteen centuries before Anno Domini Abraham left Ur in the Chaldees, and founded the Nation. Nineteen centuries after Anno Domini is the standpoint, from which we of this generation regard it.

The Christian Dispensation is *Universal* as regards mankind, and yet *Individual* as regards each Soul: it has no limitation of race, Language, Country, Time, Stage of Culture; it has no Temple, no divinely appointed Ritual, no National Feast-Days, Fast-Days, no fetters of the free Soul except those inspired by the acknowledgment of a common Father, a Universal Saviour, and an abiding Holy Spirit. The desire of the Christian is to convey what he deems the greatest of earthly treasures to others: nothing is to

him common and unclean : the slaughter of Beasts and Birds has
no relation to his views of Religion; the cleaning of pots and pans,
the incidents of dress and personal cleanliness, are nothing. Moreover, his views of things spiritual develop as Time goes on, and
embrace Humanity in its fulness, Past, Present, and Future. It
allows of difference in interpretation, and in practice: it looks
forward to no future Dispensation, but to a Resurrection, a Day of
Judgment, and Everlasting Life beyond the Grave.

The Hebrew system is narrow, and never extended beyond a few
Millions: the whole World with its Millions might perish for all
that the Hebrew cared: they were common and unclean. The
uneducated Hebrew was, in the eyes of the Priest, *accursed*. Their
hopes were limited to a miserable little Province, about the size of
two Districts of British India, a tiny town, and a Temple infini-
tesimally small in area compared with the Temples of Egypt,
Mesopotamia, and India. They cling hopelessly through long dreary
centuries to a dead Language, an obsolete Ritual, a ruined Temple :
their prayer is to be restored to a small country only able to
support four Millions, while they count to nine Millions, the restoration of the anachronism of the sacrifice of Beasts, and a temporal
Kingdom.

A remarkable paper by Claude Montefiore on the Misconceptions
of Judaism and Christianity by each other appeared in the *Jewish
Quarterly Review*, of January, 1896. Serious philosophical thinkers
are, of course, free from the prejudices of either party in favour of
their own intrinsic excellence, and against the obvious shortcomings of the other party, but the writer does not dwell sufficiently
on two points.

I. The Hebrew Dispensation was for one petty tribe only,
amidst the Millions of God's poor creatures : that tribe was in a very
low state of Culture, in an early period of the Education of the
World : the tribe had been for more than one century in the house
of bondage : it knew nothing of the great Universe, or of the outer
World of the Human race. The leader of the movement promulgated, as from God, a code of Laws, conspicuous among which were :

" Thou shalt not commit murder,"
" Thou shalt not steal,"

and yet held out to his followers as their great and everlasting
reward possession of a land, which was to be purchased by
wholesale slaughter of the unoffending occupants, very much
as Ma-Tabéle-land is occupied in this century by the Land Pirates
of British Commercial Companies. Their Worship was Ritual in
its grossest form, and was restricted to themselves.

II. The Christian Dispensation arrived at a period of great
enlightenment of the Regions of West Asia, and the Basin of the
Mediterranean : Greek Philosophy and Roman Rule had made their

mark: the new Conception was literally to be worldwide: the reward was to be in the next World.

The writer of the above-mentioned paper remarks that: (A) to the Hebrew belonged the following Conceptions: (1) God, His Love and Justice; (2) Morality not Ritual, but Conduct; (3) a desire to repress social wrongs, and develop social rights; (4) the ideal of Social Life; (5) simplicity of Doctrine; (6) Religion in every-day life. (B) To the Christian belonged: (1) the idea of the blessing of adversity; (2) the idea of Self-Sacrifice; (3) the duty to love and do good to one's enemies; (4) the idea of the Fatherhood of God; (5) freedom from ties of race; (6) subordination of Ritual to Conduct.

It is not correct to suppose, that with the History of the Hebrews commences the History of Mankind, for it is only part of the History of the elder world, and an unimportant part, when the great chart of History is unfolded. The Hebrews allowed themselves to use gross exaggeration, arising no doubt from ignorance: they talk of their Prophets as being "since the World began." But the actors on the Hebrew stage comported themselves very much as men of like passions as ourselves in a different stage of Culture: they were not prophets pulled by a string; if that had been the case, they would not have been examples for our learning.

Schopenhauer, Part I, p. 137, remarks, that the Religion of the Hebrews was the rudest of all Religions, as it had no trace of the Doctrine of the Immortality of the Soul. Bishop Warburton argues, that Moses designedly kept all reference to Life after Death in the background, that he might wean the minds of the Jews from the worship of the dead, of which they had seen so much in Egypt. Such a motive would have been a low one, and a suppression of Truth, *if he believed it to be true*. Can we suppose that if sent from God he was ignorant of this fundamental Truth, at which Zoroaster, and the Hindu Sages, had long before arrived? We know that up to the Christian era it was an open question, and the Sadducees did not believe in it.

The tendency of the Hebrew character was not so much to Idolatry, as to the entertainment of low ideas about the true God. It may have suited the Hebrews to talk about the God of Israel, as a private property, or the God of gods, as if the very existence of others than the great one God was conceivable, but we must realize, that there was a divine purpose in the existence of the Gentiles in contiguity to the Hebrews. Clement of Alexandria admits that there was a dispensation of Paganism. Bishop Westcott draws attention to Deuteronomy, iv, 19: "And lest thou lift " up thine eyes unto heaven, and when thou seest the sun, and the " moon, and the stars, even all the host of heaven, shouldest be " driven to worship them, and serve them, which the Lord thy God " hath divided unto all nations under the whole heaven." Centuries later, Paul, though a Hebrew, remarks that God did not leave Himself without a witness. It is inconceivable arrogance for the Hebrew, then, to suppose that the World was created for him, and rank folly now to imagine, that he is the heir of any peculiar privileges.

What right had Dr. Graetz to assert, that to the Hebrew race the great round World, with its fourteen hundred Millions of inhabitants, was indebted for the very conceptions of Virtue and Honour? Had he ever read Plato, or the Greek Tragedians, or Juvenal, or Seneca, or Marcus Aurelius, or Epictétus, or Zoroaster, Confucius, Buddha, and the Hindu Sages? What can exceed the line of Juvenal :

"Nil conscire sibi, nullâ pallescere culpâ"?

for, after all, Conscience is the ground-root of Virtue ; or the lines of the Hindu Sages :

"Ahinsam paramam dharmam"
("The greatest Religion is not to injure anyone")?

Had he ever read the "Noble Way" of Buddha, which consists of Altruism, or the law of Purity in those famous Sanskrit lines :

"In youth regard every woman as your mother, in middle life as your sister, in old age as your daughter"?

Did David or Solomon do so? Did the Hebrew race in their very best period conform to these elementary Laws? Their entrance into Palestine was by Murder and Robbery : their practice was Intolerance and Lust (Jeremiah, v, 8). The crucifixion of Jesus Christ, and the stoning of Stephen, were merely a continuance of their treatment of their own Prophets. Is the old Hebrew Religion in its present attenuated and maimed form still a Missionary Religion in itself, independent of its political surroundings in a free country like Great Britain? Does it embody such Spiritual Truths, absolute Truths, and such ethical Conceptions, as are adapted to the needs of the whole Human race?

Mr. Simon, in the *Jewish Quarterly Review*, July, 1893, p. 664, writes:

"He would put aside all the distinctive rites of the Hebrew,
" such as circumcision, Sabbath-day, unleavened bread, etc.: they
" may be important to the family of the Hebrews, but there are but
" two things of universal application, (1) Almsgiving, (2) Worship
" of God. Those, who lay stress upon ordinances as divinely
" ordered, do not believe them to have been enjoined to any but
" the people of Israel. The Synagogue is restricted practically to
" the Hebrew. A new place of universal Worship should be opened
" out, and in it should be set forth in what has consisted the con-
" ception of God, of Worship, of Moral Responsibility, which has

" sustained the Hebrew for two thousand years during deep afflic-
" tion. Experience is something: no people can speak of God, of
" Faith, of Prayer, with greater authority and deeper knowledge
" than the people of Israel. The time is ripe for a definite Theistic
" movement. The Hebrew represents the Necessity, and Efficacy,
" of a Life with God. There is no barrier in prayer betwixt an
" individual Human conscience and our Father. There is an un-
" speakable love on the part of the infinite Creator to His poor
" creatures. The new movement should be neither connected with
" Hebrew Ritual, nor be identical with Unitarianism. Those, who
" believe strongly, naturally wish to extend their conviction to
" others. Belief and Conversion logically involve the thought of
" a Mission."

The great reformer Mendelssohn lays great stress on the fact, that Judaism is for the *Jews*, and for no other Nation. " The Religion of my fathers *does not wish* to be extended. We are *not* to send Missions." " Our rabbis .... enjoin us to persuade, by forcible remonstrances, everyone who comes forward to be converted." " Whoever is not born conformable to our Laws, has no occasion to live according to them," he writes; and in his "Jerusalem" he presses over and over again the same idea. In point of fact, his theory seems to be, to use his own words, "that manifoldness (in Religion as in everything else) is the design and end of Provi-́dence"; and he even goes so far as to say (in reply to Laváter) " that the remote people of the Indies and Greenland are in our Religious estimation an *enviable* race."

If the Religion of the Hebrew were not meant to be extended, in what way could Israel be a benefit to the World?

One of the evidences of the vitality of a Religious Conception, is the desire to propagate it by lawful means. If the Hebrew believes, that his Religious Conception is in the right, if he admits the great principle, first introduced by Buddha into Human Morality (550 B.C.), of "Altruism," why does he not out of his great wealth organize Missions to preach to the poor Gentiles these good tidings? Has he ever done so? is not the gross right of circumcision quite sufficient to stop any attempt at spiritual conversion? Here and there I read of a poor woman being converted: can an educated man, whether Christian or Pagan, be produced, who after studying the Scriptures has accepted the Hebrew Conception, and submitted to a mutilation of his body? No doubt in the Middle Ages there was one great tribe, the Khazar, who accepted it, 740 A.D.; and a Law was passed in Russia making conversion to Judaism a penal offence, which implies that converts were made, and forbidding them to circumcise forcibly their Christian Slaves under pain of death. This Law was passed A.D. 815. When we speak harshly of forcible conversions to Islam, we must recollect these facts: and from the position, which the Hebrew pretends to occupy, he would do the same again, if he found himself strong enough to do so with impunity. ("Israel," *Encyc. Brit.*, 9th edition, vol. xiii, p. 430.)

Philo of Alexandria is credited to have held a great desire to win converts to his Religion: perhaps he was unconsciously more Hellenized than he would have liked to admit.

Now, if the Hebrew believes the Old Testament, he ought to do something to propagate the precious Truths of those Scriptures: if they are indeed the depository of God's promises, and to the Gentiles as well as the Hebrews, how can he justify his silence? Either the Hebrew race, in his opinion, was chosen as the representative of a true Religious Conception, or it was not.

In a late number of the *Jewish Quarterly Review*, Mr. Simon, a most distinguished member of the Liberal Hebrews, boldly proposes to inaugurate a Mission-policy on the part of the Hebrews to the Gentiles of London. The subject is too long to treat of here, but it seems, as if the Hebrews ought to have thought of this duty earlier in their career, and the opportunity seems to be past now: however, the experiment would be welcomed.

Intermarriage between Christian and Jew is not uncommon: some very notable cases have occurred. Hebrew writers assert that a change of Religion on the part of a Gentile universally follows marriage with a Hebrew: we can understand, that a person totally indifferent to things spiritual, merely a nominal believer, might change his or her nominal Religion without difficulty; but it is difficult to follow out the process, by which a thoughtful man or woman of ordinary Religious training, having married a Hebrew, can be persuaded to change his Religion, and adopt Liberal Judaism. The New Testament must be given up: Theism and Unitarianism must be avoided, though really they resemble Liberal Judaism very closely, the historical antiquity of the latter being the only difference: Jesus, no longer Christ, must take His place as the noblest teacher, that the world ever knew, but nothing more: feasts and fasts will have to be kept, and prayers studied in the dead Language of Hebrew. When the question of Belief is considered, it is difficult to define accurately, what the Liberal Hebrew does believe, for he must feel, that the so-called Mosaic Dispensation, so far as he is concerned, has been played out, and has failed absolutely: the promises of the Prophets have not been realized, and in his Scriptures the Hebrew finds no sure and certain prospect of a future Life: it is difficult to say on what he rests for support in discharge of his duties in this World, and what hope of reward in the next. The *Jewish Quarterly Review* informs the public, that young women accept Judaism on the occasion of marriage: no one can take a serious view of a spiritual conversion as the accompaniment of matrimony. I make the following extract from a Periodical:

"CONVERTS TO JUDAISM.—An announcement has just been published to the effect, that the Jewish ecclesiastical authorities, the Beth Din, will in future permit the induction of Christians, and others, in the Jewish faith. It is among the things not generally known, that from the admission of the Jews into England during the Commonwealth to the present time not one Gentile of either sex has been received into the Anglo-Jewish community by English rabbis or Jewish ministers resident in this country. Englishmen have, of course, embraced Hebrew doctrines from time to time; but conversion does not necessarily mean submission to rites. Every year, however, a considerable number of Christian women have gone over to Holland, Belgium, and France, and have there renounced Christianity in favour of the more ancient faith, the rabbis in these countries being under no obligation to refuse to induct proselytes. These converts are generally young women, and in ninety-nine cases out of a hundred they change for matrimonial reasons. Not many care to marry out of their pale at all, and when they do they naturally wish their wives to be formally received. The reason why the spiritual chiefs of the community have declined up till now to receive proselytes can be traced to the time of the Commonwealth, when it was imagined by the ignorant and the bigoted, that the Hebrew sought admission to this country in order to gain adherents to their Religion. To banish this delusion the rabbis of the time engaged themselves, under heavy penalties, to refuse admission to the synagogue of any Christian. And this rule, enacted by Israelites for Israelites, has remained in force from the time of Menasseh Ben Israel to that of the Rev. Dr. Adler. That the Hebrew in our own day do not wish to begin the business of conversion, we may be well assured. The truth is, that some of the most influential members of the Hebrew community have during the last three or four years taken unto themselves Christian wives; some noble Jewesses have made themselves happy with Gentile husbands; and it happens, that Hebrews rarely maintain the rites and obligations of their faith after they have married out of it. The readiness of Dr. Adler and his coadjutors, therefore, to save intending proselytes the expense and trouble of a journey to Holland or Belgium, may be traced to mixed marriages."

And when attempts are made to bring to their notice the tenets of another Religion, not by force, not by temptation of worldly profit, but simply from motives of unselfish benevolence, and in the way of friendly argument, the Hebrew draws up, and is offended, and assumes the airs of a rich man, to whom a penny by way of Charity is offered.

In a lecture in the Temple Israel, apropos of the movement to convert Hebrews, Dr. Harris remarked:

" To send Missionaries to convert us, is an insult to our faith and
" to us. We are not barbarians; we are not besotted revellers;
" we know what Duty is, none better. Come to us to learn
" Religion, if you will, but not to teach it. In the field of
" Religion we are the masters, 'the witnesses of God,' and the
" World has sat at our feet.

" I say, that Christians insult us more, when they patronize us,
" than when they persecute us. Let them kill us, if they will,
" as they are doing in Russia, but let them not send their
" Missionaries to save us. I say that we are being perpetually
" humiliated, and more by our would-be friends than by our
" open foes.

" I hold that to disturb a man's faith is about the most awful
" thing that man can do. To tell him that his soul is lost, cursed
" of God, because he believes in the faith of his fathers, I would
" shrink from it.

" What have they to offer for this? What do they know that
" we do not? Our people are temperate. Drunkards are not as
" numerous as among Christians. The sanctity of the home is
" maintained. The Jews love home; they are a thriving people;
" they have the energy to make valuable citizens. Will the
" Missionaries be able to make them any better? Compare two
" congregations, one of Jews and one of Christians, in sobriety,
" industry, and morality.

" We must insist, that our Christian neighbours treat us with
" equality. We must insist, that they cease to treat us, as if we
" were African barbarians. We must insist, that they treat us
" as their fellow-citizens. We ask simply, that they treat us with
" such dignity, as we are entitled to.

" It is hard enough to be blackballed at the clubs, but then
" to be defended in the Christian pulpit on the following Sunday,
" and to be informed, that we are quite respectable people, that is
" intolerable. Some of us, unfortunately, have not sufficient self-
" respect, and feel flattered, when we ought to feel indignant.

" Therefore to our friends, as to our enemies, I say, ' Let us
" alone.' Let us train our children to understand that, wherever
" they may go, their presence confers honour quite as decidedly as
" it receives it. To those amiable but narrow partisans, who,
" anxious about our souls, contribute liberally toward Jewish
" Missionaries, let me say: ' Devote your zeal and your purses
" to more worthy and less thankless causes.' For the Jew to
" renounce Monotheism, a belief in one sole God, and to accept
" a belief in a Triune God, is a step backward. Even progressive
" Christianity, in its latest and highest development, Unitarianism,
" has gradually dropped this last remnant of Paganism."

The African Barbarian has a common ground with the Hebrew,

which Dr. Harris omits to notice. Both mutilate their bodies under the idea, that it is an index of the relation of their Soul to their great Creator. But is the discoverer of a mine of gold to be blamed, if he publishes the good news, and invites the whole World to share the benefit of his discovery? The Hebrew is not compelled by the Arm of the Flesh to change his time-honoured Conceptions: all that is done is, to lay before his educated Intellect, and his awakened Spirituality, a new way of seeking for God, if haply He can be found; and, if the Hebrew undertakes in the same spirit to publish the tenets of his ancient Faith, and to expound the merits of his practices, e.g., Sacrifice of Animals, Restriction of the Mercies of the common God to one petty race, Prayers in an unknown Language, Mutilation of the male body, Slaughter of cattle in a manner, which causes unnecessary pain to the poor animals for a reason, which it is ridiculous to state, eating unleavened bread, etc., his arguments will receive respectful attention, and perhaps, as often happens to the Christian Missionary, while expounding his doctrines to others, he will more fully realize the nature of the doctrines and practices of the Elder World, which he is expounding, and ask himself: "Are these things true? Is it possible, that our eyes are blinded, and that we do not see the presence of God everywhere during all the ages, and the progress of the capacity of the Soul of Man to understand Him."

It would appear, that the very *raison d'être*, and prime motive, of the Hebrew Dispensation has passed away: no one can doubt, that its first and great object was to enforce the principle of Monotheism, and denounce the Worship under any pretence of graven Images, with which the Hebrews became so familiar in Egypt. No one can say, that at the present Epoch Polytheism, and Idolatry, are the prevailing spiritual evils. The great majority of mankind, thanks to Christianity, Islam, Buddhism, Zoroastrianism, and Confucianism, have outgrown this weakness, which survives in the Brahmanical Conception, and was notorious in the old Semitic Religious Conceptions, the Graeco-Roman, Egyptian, and Mesopotamian, Conceptions and Cults. The Human race is now not in danger of serving many gods, but in denying the existence of any God.

But such is the weakness of the Human race, that germs of this old primeval error crop up, notably in the Greek and Roman forms of Christianity, in Buddhism and Confucianism, and, strange to say, in the Hebrew Dispensation. The cultus of the Temple in the Post-Exilic Period became to the Hebrew a kind of Worship, *an end in itself*: the idea obtained, that a perpetual maintenance of Temple-Worship would secure the favour of a satisfied Deity: it was performed as much for God's glory, as for the spiritual benefit of the sinful worshipper. The Temple became a perpetual Divine Manifestation, a place, where the Deity actually resided, and in its utter destruction we read the lesson, that God dwelleth not in temples made with hands. The destruction of the Hebrews as a Nation showed, that their Mission had been performed.

Other Religious Conceptions have no Geographical limits assigned to them, notably the Buddhist, Christian, and Mahometan: they are universal in place and race. The great Brahmanical Conception is absolutely localized in India, and limited to the inhabitants of that vast Region. A thoughtful Hindu remarked to me with an expression of satisfaction, worthy of a Hebrew, that he could become a Christian, whenever he liked, but that no earthly power could enable me to become a Hindu. I had to be thankful for small mercies, and was grateful for this disability. At any rate, the Hindu-Sthan, and Arya-Dés, or "place of the Hindu," is still occupied by them in 200 Millions, but the very *raison d'être* of the Hebrew has disappeared for eighteen centuries: one of their promises was not Everlasting Life, but "that their days might be long in the land, which the Lord thy God giveth thee." Their great Lawgiver never saw the Promised Land except by a far-off view from Mount Pisgah. Over and over again they were warned, that their tenure of the Land was dependent on their maintenance of Monotheism, and the sole Worship of Jehovah; and yet they went whoring after other gods, the miserable abomination of neighbouring tribes. It is clear, therefore, that, when their day of reckoning came, they lost their Land, and their Dispensation, as far as Human eyes can see, has come to an end.

How different would have been their effect and influence on the Graeco-Roman World in the dawn of its greatness, if within the Holy Land there had been a Holy People, strictly adhering to their Holy Law, not the letter only, the anise and cumin, but to the Spirit, Purity of Soul, Obedience to the Law, and a Desire by Human Love to extend this Blessing to their fellow-men. The Hebrew had a distinct Mission then, both in Palestine and Egypt, and Babylon, and in every place, where Moses was read on the Sabbath. A blindness came upon Israel. Had the new Dispensation been made by a Greek, or a Roman, or an Egyptian, they might have resisted it from mere Chauvinism, but it came from a Hebrew of the line of David, with the Hebrew Scriptures on His lips: and they refused to hear Him.

The Hebrew race has been hardly dealt with by everyone, with whom they came into contact since the time that Jacob went down into Egypt. They were led to believe, that they were somehow or other the chosen people of the Creator of the Universe, though they knew Him only as the God of their own Nation, and quite admitted the (to our notions) inconceivable idea of there being gods of other Nations: Psalm xcv, 3, places this beyond doubt: "For the Lord is a great God, *and a great king above all gods.*" In any other Nation of antiquity, and in Christian parlance, He would have been called, and is called, the God: but to call him "the king above other gods," who never existed, means nothing: Zeus might have been called so, but Yahveh never.

I have dwelt upon the insignificance of the kingdom of David. All the stories of Solomon's wisdom and wealth are mere exaggerations: his wealth is far exceeded by that of Rothschild; as to his wisdom, it is exceeded by Spinoza, and a row of learned Israelites of modern days. The Hebrew Nation achieved greatness in nothing. India, China, Japan, Persia, Assyria, Babylonia, and Egypt, looked on them with scorn; some of them had never heard of their name. In those days they could not cope with the Greeks in Philosophy, or with the Romans in organization, or even Morals. Mordecai sold his niece to be a member of a king's Harem: Virginius preferred to slay his daughter to save her from a life of shame.

With all this they were habitually false to their God Yahveh. Jeremiah v places this beyond doubt: they were fearfully immoral, exceptionally cruel, terribly unfaithful, going after the so-called gods of neighbouring tribes: one king went one way, his son another: they were intolerant to a degree, and yet always expected toleration for themselves. They were swept into exile; a few, a very few, counting by hundreds, came back, having lost their Language, and their independence, whatever they understood by Prophets, had ceased: a volume of written Law had been got together, to which they gave a servile obedience, to the letter, not the spirit. They were transferred from the rule of the Persian Monotheists to the Greek Polytheists, and from them to the Roman Polytheists. They insisted on the interpretation of Ancient Prophecies, that a temporal Redeemer would come, but twenty-five centuries have passed away, and a temporal Redeemer has not come: they fondly anticipated a restoration of the petty kingdom of their Shepherd-King David in his little town of Jerusalem, as if it had been an ancient Monarchy and a vast city, which had ruled other Nations for centuries, like the great Dynasties in Egypt or Mesopotamia.

The migration of the Hebrews from Egypt has its parallel in the great migration of the Mongols from the country round the mouth of the Volga into Central Asia, or the migration of the Mormonites into the Salt Lake Region. Centuries later the return of the Hebrews from Babylon was an epoch-making event in the History of the World, and its outcome was advantageous to the whole Human race. It was not only a solemn event in the History of the Hebrews, but the solution of a question of Life and Death to future generations. Had a portion of the tribes of Judah and Benjamin not returned from captivity, their fate would have in the course of time been that of their brethren of the Ten Tribes: they would have disappeared in the quagmire of conquered Nations; their individuality would have faded away: Christianity would never have come into existence, as the Hebrew Books would have disappeared;

and later centuries would have known nothing of those strange Hebrew legends, which have charmed and consoled so many generations of men. The little caravan, which crossed the Desert 535 B.C. from Babylon to Jerusalem, carried with it the Future of the Religions of the World, and laid the foundation of the greatest Spiritual Conception of the Human race.

It must be an additional aggravation to the Hebrew to hear, how the Precious Promises made to his race to Israel by name, are appropriated through a poetic license and a daring figuration, by Christian Gentiles. It has been well said, that the Prophecies, Promises, and Prayers, of the Old Testament teach us, that the fundamental purpose of the Election and Preservation of Israel was, that it should become a channel and instrument of blessing to the entire World; but the Preacher should discontinue the practice of spiritualizing all Promises to Israel, and appropriating them to Christians, while literalizing all threatenings, and applying them to Israel alone. If Israel be indeed a type of God's dealings with the whole World, it is so both for Punishment as well as Blessing. Israel's place to the reflecting and thinking World is not what the Hebrew himself presumed to think in the time of the Kingdom, nor what our forefathers in their ignorance were taught to believe. The present generation knows, that all mankind since the day of the Creation of Man are God's children, made in His Image, and God has loved them all, and hated nothing that He has made. If He chose the Hebrew out of the rest of His poor children (passing by the learned Egyptians, Babylonians, Indians, and Chinese, who even then were great, and powerful, and learned) to be the custodians of His Oracles, and the channel of His Grace to the World, as through one of their race the great Incarnation was to take place, their faithless, rebellious, and idolatrous, conduct before the Exile, and their unspiritual ritualistic Worship after the Exile, show how little worthy they were of the high honour conferred upon them. When they are weighed in the balance with the great Nations, who were their contemporaries, they are found to have left no contribution to the sum-total of Human Knowledge, and only a darkened view of Divine Knowledge.

At the time of our Lord the number of Hebrews and Proselytes, dwelling outside the limits of Judea, far exceeded the number of those, who had access to the Temple Sacrifice, or went up to the Annual Feasts. If any of the Diasporà went up to Jerusalem, it was as great an effort in their time as a Pilgrimage to Mekka is to a Mahometan dwelling in India. It follows, that to the majority of the Diasporà the rite of Sacrifice had practically ceased: many passed through life, even in the days of Paul, without ever making a Sacrifice: the Synagogue-Ritual and Prayers had, by the slow process of events, replaced the Temple-slaying of Beasts, and, when the Temple was destroyed, it made no difference to the Worship of the Diasporà.

Spinoza remarks, that the Jews maintained their independent social position not only in spite of, but in consequence of, the persecution, which they most unjustly met at the hands of Christian Gentiles: what possible connection could the millions of the Diasporà in every city of the Roman Empire have with the Crucifixion at Jerusalem? Yet it was the hatred, which arose falsely from this event, which preserved their individuality: they never disappeared and melted away like the Ten Tribes in Mesopotamia. It is possible, that their present so-called emancipation, and the levelling hand of Civilization and National Culture, may lead to their absorption, when the process extends beyond the Political to the Social sphere. We have an indication of this in what we see around us in the higher classes of Hebrews in Europe. In 1500 A.D., when Reuchlin, the first European Hebrew Scholar, wished to lecture on that Language at Heidelberg, the Priests of Rome objected on the ground, that the Hebrews were an accursed people, who had crucified the Lord, and anyone, who made use of their Language, was a heretic: when they were reminded that the Old Testament was in Hebrew, they retorted that the Latin Vulgate was the only Bible of the Church. Things are changed now.

Conclusion.

Our plain duty is to do our best to bring the simple doctrine of Christ Crucified, and Christ Risen, to the hearts of the survivors of His race: this is not the place to describe this policy, but merely to state it: it is no new idea, but as old as the time of Paul of Tarsus. *But there our Duty ends.* We are not in the least called upon to admit any superiority in Grace and Election of the Jew to the Gentile: the two terms in this special significance have ceased to exist. And really, the obsolete customs, and insignificant History, of this petty tribe should no longer be introduced into the serious discussion of the most important problems of Human Life. The Sacred Books of the Hebrew were written by individuals, and for a people, in a state of Barbarism, without Science, or Arts, Commerce with Foreign Nations, or any knowledge of the History, Geography, or even existence, of the outer World: there were none of the checks on the writer of a public Press, or an educated critical class: there was most conventional phraseology, grossness of expression, and wild utterance. We accept those Books gratefully; they have a charm of their own. We love the utterances of the Greek, Latin, and Sanskrit, writers for the same reason: we seem to hold converse with the great and wise men of old, and bow our heads to them across the abyss of centuries. But all that the Hebrews wrote is totally out of the environment of modern argument, and has no practical relation to the stream of modern life: it is mere pulpit-euphemism, or rhetorical flourish, and should be abandoned, when the discussion is serious, on the relation of God to the Souls of His poor creatures, the whole Human race, as I wish this discussion to be.

It has never been given to any other Nation but the Hebrew to express openly and unreservedly, during a long series of years, their conviction in the coming in some dim and remote period of a great Personage of their own race and Nation, who would restore their fallen fortunes; and in the fulness of time that Personage arrived. No other Literature presents so striking a phenomenon. No prophecy foretold the coming of Buddha, or Socrates, the only names, which can be mentioned in the same breath with Jesus of Nazareth. The most superficial reader of the Old Testament cannot fail to mark the golden thread, which entwines itself throughout the texture of ancient Hebrew Literature. The Hebrew thinks, that the promised Messiah has not yet come : Nineteen centuries is a long time to wait, especially as the Country, the Nationality, the Language, the local customs, have all passed away. Can we doubt, that through all the pages of these Ancient Books from the time of Abraham, there is a finger pointing to the time of appearance of some one ? The indication is indeed not clear, and the truth is concealed by fanciful interpretations. Since a certain date, a date, from which all Modern History counts, there has been a deep silence, and certain Prophecies have been unmistakably fulfilled. How does the Hebrew explain this fact away ?

Let anyone, who really has accepted the Christian Dispensation, and has *a personal Knowledge of Christ*, and his precious Promises, close his eyes, and reflect upon what I have written *ex animo* in these three Essays, and then open his eyes again, and imagine the mere possibility of that one great central Figure, the object of the Faith, Hope, and Love, of countless millions, having disappeared from the Picture of Human affairs in the same way as Asher, Amen Ra, and Zeus, by the lapse of time, and the widening of Human Knowledge, have disappeared. Can the Conception of the Son of God, who assumed Human Form, and died for the sins of all His Human Brethren, and reconciled them to His Father, and their Father, be surpassed in Fulness, and Sufficiency, in Universality, and Opportuneness, in Suitability to the weaknesses and wants of the Human race, by any, Past or Present, Religious Conception ? The Future is with God.

The end of the matter, is this : any rights, that a citizen of the great Nations of Europe and America possesses, should be, or have been, conceded to a Hebrew without any possible exception, and the most entire Tolerance to their peculiar Religious views or customs, so long as they are not in antagonism to the Moral standards of the Nineteenth century. When we recall the cruel wrongs done to their forefathers in past centuries, we should be disposed to render more kindness, restitution, if possible, of buildings torn from them, compensation for confiscations, every possible Educational, Constitutional, and Social, Privilege, and something beyond in token of Regret for the Past, and in atonement for the sins of our Ancestors.

As regards attempts to bring to their notice the Gospel of Jesus Christ, it is the duty of Christians in every lawful way to do so, and the Hebrew is quite at liberty to press upon his fellow-citizens his own Religious views in any way, which may appear desirable to him. By maintaining such a base custom, as mutilation of the male body, as a token of spiritual Conversion, killing animals for food in a way calculated to increase suffering, and observing a different day of weekly rest from his fellow-citizens, he must feel, that he is in a miserable minority, and must put up with the consequence of being out of harmony and touch with the lawful and unobjectionable practices of his Epoch, and place of habitation.

If he has hopes for the Future, after nearly two thousand years of expatriation and denationalization, he is perfectly at liberty to entertain them, but they are outside of practical consideration; and by putting them forward he only makes himself an object of pity, and to the thoughtless of ridicule. The men, who uttered and committed to paper those Promises, on which he founds his hopes, were men utterly ignorant of Geography, History, the physical Laws of the Universe, which were the same then as now; they were devoid of all Culture, all sense of responsibility; they spoke to contemporaries more ignorant than themselves; they partook more of the character of Preachers than Predictors. No such utterances in modern times would be listened to by the most ignorant. All the great Truths, which they promulgated, of Monotheism, the duty of man to his Creator, and Morality, are admitted on all sides. The existence of the petty tribes of the Hebrews may have had some motive, some part to play, in the progress of the World *then*: *it has none now*. The great Religious Conceptions, in the midst of which they came into existence, with all the old-world paraphernalia of Sacrifice, Prophecy, Miracles, Auguries, Dreams, Signs from Heaven, Visions, have passed away: I do not stop to discuss, whether there was Truth, or a *raison d'être* in them *then*: they have passed away *now*, and yet the same God rules the World now as then, and is worshipped in Spirit and Truth, and the presence of His Holy Spirit cannot be denied as immanent in all His poor creatures.

The $\mu\acute{v}\theta o\iota$, or myths, of the early periods of a Nation are not necessarily false: they appear to have been the modes, in which in the early stage of Human Culture great Truths were enunciated, and recorded, and we can safely admit, that they were to that extent from God (Gore's "Lux Mundi," 5th edition, pp. 356, 357, and Preface, pp. xxviii, xxix), but there is a limit of time to their value, for the centre of action of Human environment has been changed:

the Earth is no longer the most important feature of the Universe, Nor is the Hebrew race in any possible sense the pivot, on which the development of mankind ever turned, or does now turn: these fond and foolish notions must be abandoned.

To assert, that the Hebrew has a Mission still unfulfilled, except as to his own Conversion to a more intelligent Faith, cannot be admitted: to assert, that his Morality was at any period of his existence higher than that, which was promulgated by the great Seekers after God, and Teachers of Mankind of Ancient and Modern Time, cannot be admitted by those, who have studied the Sacred Books of all Religious Conceptions, and the History of the Human race. In all the writers on the Hebrew Nation, a marked ignorance is evidenced of the History of the Ancient Nations of Asia, North Africa, and Europe, and an absence of the study of their Sacred and Philosophical Books, though they are accessible in the three great Languages of Europe, English, French, and German.

Of what possible use is the prolonged existence in isolation of the Hebrew people, who realize, as stated in Section I, the conditions neither of Nation nor race? Are they the leaven of a new and higher Religious Conception in any of the countries, in which they have obtained the position of citizens, honoured, wealthy, learned in every branch of Science, and every Art? In the Senate, in the Courts of Law, in the Universities, in Commerce, in the Halls of the Scientist, they represent a great Power as regards things of this World; there are among them some of the greatest, the best, and the sweetest, of men, whose genius and acquirements claim the highest admiration, and obtain it; but, still, their Religious Conception is a survival of a Dead Past, with no promise of a Living Future.

Did, then, no profit to the Human race arise from the Hebrew Conception? Much every way, chiefly because to men of their race were revealed in a most unmistakable manner the Counsels of God: and their voices are still heard. Still, to the Hebrew alone was committed those writings, called by one of the greatest and wisest of men, Paul the Hebrew, "the Oracles of God."

And so long as Human hearts beat, love must be extended to that one family among the families of Nations, of which came Jesus of Nazareth in the fulness of time. Just at the period, when the parting of the ways was about to take place, the existence of the Hebrew was of unique and overpowering advantage.

I quote words from one of my former volumes, "Common Features which appear in all forms of Belief," 1895, p. 65:

"The Palestinian Hebrew in the century preceding Anno
" Domini had fallen to the lowest level of empty Ritual. The
" destruction of the Temple, and the cessation of the Mosaic form
" of Worship, were at hand. In the meantime, the Hebrew of the
" Diasporà was supplying the leaven of Progress to all the races,

" and Nations, with whom he came into contact. He had no
" Temple, no Priesthood, no Ritual; but he had a high Ideal, and
" he was unconsciously preparing a platform in every city of
" West Asia, North Africa, and Europe, on which the new
" Religious Conception could rest: the kingdom of Israel, and the
" old Jerusalem, were ready to disappear. The shadow of the 'King-
" dom of God' [and of 'Heaven' (for it is called by both names)],
" and the New Jerusalem, fell on the slide of the great Lantern of
" the Universe. Moses was read in every Synagogue every Sabbath.
" A few years later Christ was to be read also, for it may roughly
" be said, that where there was a Synagogue, there would soon be
" a Church. Primitive Christianity sprang up in a soil prepared
" by two or three centuries of Hebrew Culture. The Jew of the
" Diasporà, deprived of means of access to the outward centre of
" his hereditary Worship, arrived at the conviction, that his call
" was to serve God in a pure manner, and observe the principles
" of his Religion, since he was hopelessly debarred from the
" Ritual."

Nothing apparently was more destructive of the spirituality of the Hebrew Religion than the Deuteronomic precept of there being only one place of Worship for the sons of Abraham in the petty town conquered by David from the Jebusites, and in which his son had by the help of Heathen workmen from Tyre erected his little Temple, for we have only to compare the extent of its area, which can be traced with certainty, with that of the temples in Egypt, and Baelbek in Syria, to be convinced how small and unimportant as a building it was. Yet the centralization of Ritual led to the extinction of local and family Worship: there were no Synagogues then; there could be no family, or parochial, altar: once a year those, who were strong, and had the means, could make a painful pilgrimage to the solitary place of Worship of a country as large as Belgium, and amidst the excitement, suffering, and exhaustion of the journey sacrifice their beast, and troop back. We can see how it was in the time of our Lord's childhood, when He was lost in the crowd. We in India all know what a Pilgrimage is, and how many never live to get home, and how the modern Railway nowadays helps a pious heathen to get with his family to his Idol-Temple. Religion would have died out in Palestine, had it not been supplemented by the Synagogue, and in the Diasporà the Synagogue was the centre of the Religion, free from Sacrifice, or debased Ritual. Other Nations are glad to forget the events connected with their barbarous and often cruel infancy. As a fact the existence of a Nation is built on the blood and bones of the one, which preceded it, just as in the Syrian Tell at Lachish the layer of each superimposed town unmistakably, though silently, tells of the slaughter of the inhabitants by force or treachery of the layer next below. All the cruel details elsewhere are forgotten; but the

Hebrews delight to record all such atrocities committed by their forefathers, and thousands of years afterwards to read them aloud, as a form of Worship in their Synagogue. Moreover, the shocking cruelty of killing all men, women, and children, of an inoffensive tribe, and reserving all the adult virgins for the convenience of the conquerors, is attributed to the commands of the Great Creator of all mankind, who loved the whole World. It is often forgotten, that the tribes, whom they thus slaughtered, were their near kinsmen on the side of their maternal ancestors, as eleven of the sons of Jacob had married women of Canaan, and the Language, which they spoke, was called the Language of Canaan (Isaiah, xix, 18).

I quote from Eber's "Only a Word," p. 85, the expressions of a learned, gentle, and persecuted Jew, as putting the matter of giving up their ancestral Religion in another light, one in which we can all sympathize:

"Christ's love embraced all Nations: He loved all mankind: my "Soul thirsts to help my fellow-men, but they have never ceased "to crush me and my people in our efforts to be good in the fullest "sense of their own Master's teaching: the Christian refuses this "to the Jew: if I dare to treat a Christian as a fellow-creature "what would my fate be? The Jew is not to be good: the men, "who lay that burden on their brethren's shoulders, incur such "guilt as I know no pardon for: if Jesus Christ were to return to "the World, and see the pack, that hunts us down, He would open "His arms wide to embrace us."

The atrocious conduct of Christian Governments, peoples, and individuals has done a wrong to the Hebrew, which can never be expiated. How has it happened, that it seems part of our nature to be averse to the very race, of which the Lord of Life came? We feel it, though we would not injure them, and pity those of our fellows, who have Hebrew blood in their veins. No wonder the Hebrew feels it more deeply, and, when he accepts Christ, he still is unwilling to enter into any Gentile Association. We hardly lay sufficient stress on the influence of this feeling, that, though they become Christians in Religion, they have not ceased to be Hebrews in race, as if it were a great inheritance: they are proud of an origin, which unconsciously seems to the Gentile anything but a cause of pride.

How much greater would have been the image of the Hebrew in the page of History of after ages, if it had died away after giving birth to the great Universal Religious Conception, which now fills so large a part in the spiritual life of the sons of men! It might, indeed, have lived in its unbroken and annually increasing Millions in its own country, the place of its birth, like the Brahmanical Religion of India, which, after giving birth to the great Universal Religion of Buddha, still retains one-seventh of the population of the Globe in its fold: but the Hebrew has been ignominiously driven out of the petty Province, which was given, according to his story, to him by the Almighty as an everlasting possession. His great form of adoration by Sacrifice of Beasts has ceased for 1,800 years: the last Passover-Lamb has been slaughtered in the Holy of Holies; the last bullock in the outer court of the Temple. The Hebrews were chosen to be the servants of the Lord, but their Dispensation has proved an entire failure: they *have nothing to show to justify their existence* since the time of the Maccabees. Fallen as the Greeks are, they still retain their Cities and their Language: no one has superseded Plato and Aristotle: the very words uttered by their great Dramatists still ring in our ears; the very words, which entranced an Athenian audience seated in the Theatre of Bacchus under the hill of the Parthenon, where the Temple of Athens still looks down in its serene beauty; it was 400 years older than Herod's temple at Jerusalem, every stone of which is gone. The Greek Religious Conception has passed away, because its work was done, and the minds of men have passed to higher things. But, like the remnant of the Religion of Zoroaster, which still survives in India, a remnant of the Hebrew Religion, which came under the patronage of the Persian King at Babylon, still maintains a moribund, profitless existence, appealing to a Past, but with no hope for a Future; and what profit is there in a Religious Conception, so devoid of the Spirit of Altruism, so wrapped up in Selfish Egoism, that it cares not for the Millions outside its miserable fold, and takes no part in stemming the inroad of Atheism, and Agnosticism, and the back-tide of Paganism, which threaten to overwhelm the World?

August, 1897.

IV.

The Superior Excellence of a Religious Conception, evidenced by the Results.

(1) A calm, and fearless, and unsparing, comparison of its tenets with those of every other Conception, Past, Present, or dimly visioned in the Future, when purified from the degrading survivals of previous Religious Conceptions of the race.

(2) The unconquerable desire of those, who believe in it, to extend it to other races, and the whole of mankind, by peaceful argument, unselfish sacrifice, and inducements wholly free from carnal advantages.

Section 1.

In this series of Essays we are weighing Religious Conceptions on their own fundamental merits, quite apart from the accretions of Ritual and Dogma, which have clung to them, and the evil customs and habits of those, who profess to believe them, though these two features are, rightly or wrongly, imputed to the Religious Conception.

We ask ourselves dispassionately, philosophically, and, as far as we can, truthfully, without prejudice, without partiality, what did our forefathers, in the History of the World, have presented to them as to,

(1) The relation of the Soul to the Great Creator.
(2) The Conception of this Creator, as far as limited Human Thought can deal with the Infinite.
(3) The whole duty of Man, during the term of mortal life, to Himself, his fellow-men, and his Creator.
(4) The spirit, in which he should patiently bear the ills of life, and temperately enjoy the pleasures.
(5) The submissive feelings, in which Death is to be met, and the degree of certainty of a Future State of Rewards and Punishments beyond the Grave.

On these subjects, taking them chronologically,

(1) What did the Egyptian profess? (See Essay I.)
(2) What did the Assyrian profess? (See Essay I.)
(3) What did the Hindu Sages profess? (See Essay I.)
(4) What did Moses profess? (See Essay III.)
(5) What did Zoroaster profess? (See Essay III.)
(6) What did Gautama Buddha profess? (Well known.)
(7) What did Socrates and Plato profess? (Well known.)

To those, who complacently ignore the Spiritual History of the World, and in their deep ignorance consider, that the great Creator had been for long centuries out of possession of his own Creation, and had left the millions of His poor creatures for fifty generations of men to the unconditional control of Satan, we have only one reply:

"God so loved the World (the whole World) that He sent His only Son," etc.
"God hated nothing, that He had made."
"God does not willingly afflict the Children of Men."

We recognize His presence in all the ages, at all times, in all circumstances. By a breath of His will, He could have made all men Christians on Creation's dawn, and given them the true Knowledge, just in the same way, that He gave them the gift of Language to communicate with their fellows, and a Religious Instinct to enable them to feel after God. Men are very much the same in their natures, but their peculiar characteristics are formed by their environment. We Englishmen would have thought, spoken, and acted, very much as the Egyptians and Assyrians, if we had come into the World at that Epoch of the World's History, on that round of Human Culture, in that degree of Ignorance of Things Physical, and Things Spiritual. We must stand apart from our Nineteenth-century arrogant environment, and not only consider the circumstances of other Nations in past ages, but try humbly to

"Justify the ways of God to man."

From the point of view, from which some modern Missionaries regard the present state of three-fourths of the Human race, the Wisdom, the Justice, and the Love, the inexhaustible Love, of the great Father, are called into question. Can the Ruler of the earth act without a plan in the control of the destiny of His poor creatures, whom He has condescended to make, with a Soul in His own image, and a body only somewhat physically above the beasts that perish. It was all very well for the ignorant Hebrews at the time of the Exodus to imagine, that the great Creator only cared for them, and hated the Egyptians. We know better now. Every good and every perfect gift is from above: all that Science, and Art, and Genius, can produce, are emphatically "ἄωρα Θεόυ," "the gifts of God." Consider the part in ancient History played by the Egyptian, the Assyrian, the Persian, the Indian, and the Greek, and contrast with it the miserable example, set by the tiny tribe of the Hebrews, self-condemned by their own History, called a generation of vipers by John the Baptist, condemned in the most scathing terms by the Son of God, and utterly swept out of the list of Nations by the Romans 1,800 years ago.

In the fulness of Time came that Son of God. It would seem, as if the Divine Plan had been to educate the Nations of Asia, Europe, and North Africa by sending at different times different Messengers, Παιδάγωγοι, to lead them to a just appreciation of the great problem of Existence. We have now in our Libraries the concentrated Wisdom of the elder World, "The Sacred Books": we can judge, how far Mankind had advanced in the great School, in which they were to learn the Nature of God, and the Duty of Man. We pity the intellect and spiritual deficiency of the person, who can read the words of Plato, of Buddha, of Zoroaster, of Confucius, and of the Hindu Sages; who can spell out the Papyri of Egypt, and the baked bricks of Mesopotamia, all of which have been marvellously preserved, and not feel that by a great Miracle a silent voice is heard through a Telephone from the grave, calling out, that there were men of wisdom, of worth, of power to appreciate the Divinity of God, centuries before the self-sufficient, narrow-minded, Theologian of Mediaeval Europe came into existence.

If the Mediaeval Christians had known of their existence, they would have condemned them to the same fate, to which Pagan Emperors in past ages, and Romish Priests in modern times, condemn the Christian Scriptures when circulated in the Vernacular, and the Church of Rome condemned the writings of all who presumed to differ from them, creating the great "My Doxy" or "Orthodox" party; but the "Your Doxy" or "Allodox" party are now able to get a hearing, and students of the Nineteenth century humbly think, that they are able to take a wider view of the dealings of God with the Human race than was possible to the limited opportunities of obtaining information available to the Bishops of Carthage and Hippo in North Africa, and of Rome and Constantinople in Europe. To this generation the whole World is thrown open, and we doubt not, that the Twentieth century will sit in severe judgment on our failings and errors.

I have lately, in an Essay presented to the International Oriental Congress held at Geneva in 1894, gone over in detail with cold impartiality all the Ethical or Book-Religious Conceptions of the Elder World before the great Anno Domini: this Essay is reprinted in my "Linguistic and Oriental Essays," Series IV, pp. 408–431.

Of the Religious Conceptions of the World Past and Present we know something, and can class them from different points of view.

Three of these are Universal and Propagandist, and admit into their fold all God's creatures, without reference to race or Nationality, and on perfect equality:

    I. Buddhism, 550 B.C.
    II. Christianity, the great Anno Domini.
    III. Islam, 622 A.D.

Two of the Ancient Religious Conceptions gave birth to a mighty offspring greater than themselves, and totally opposed to their Parents:

  I. The Hindu Religious Conception gave birth, B.C. 550, to the Buddhist.
  II. The Hebrew Religious Conception gave birth to the Christian at the Christian era, and from both sprang (indirectly) Islam, 622 A.D.

Two of the Ancient Religious Conceptions of the World deny the existence of any God, and are practically atheistical:

  I. The Confucianist of China, 550 B.C.
  II. The Buddhist, 550 B.C.

This appears to me to disqualify them absolutely from being acceptable to Mankind in the Nineteenth century; at any rate, they lie outside the scope of my inquiry.

Four of the Ancient Religious Conceptions of the World are dead:

  I. The Mesopotamian.
  II. The Egyptian.
  III. The Graeco-Roman.
  IV. The Teutonic, Keltic, Slavonic.

Two of the Ancient Religious Conceptions seem but miserable, and profitless, survivals, of what was great and influential in former centuries, but entirely out of touch with the environment of Modern Culture, and not likely to advance the Salvation of Mankind:

  I. The Zoroastrian or Parsi.
  II. The Hebrew.

There remain, therefore, but three Theistic, and effective, Religious Conceptions:

  I. The Brahmanical.
  II. The Christian.
  III. The Mahometan.

It is unnecessary to notice the Animistic Conceptions of Savage, and Barbarian, Tribes, nor does it lie within the scope of this Essay to notice the Sectarian Subdivisions of each of these great Conceptions. I also omit, as unworthy of serious notice from my point of view, Jainism in India, Taouism in China, and Shintoism in Japan.

There is no subject, on which mere Religionists, as distinguished from impartial inquirers into the facts evidenced by History, lose all sense of impartiality and justice, as in their opinions formed of the characteristics, merits, and demerits, the strong and weak sides, of Religious Conceptions of other people. If Christians, they take the lofty standard of their own Books, and compare it with the lamentable and degraded *practice* of the followers of other Conceptions, forgetting that the comparison should be of (1) the Precepts of the one with the Precepts of the other, and (2) the Practice of Christians with the Practice of non-Christians.

In modern Missionary Reports the story is always told from the Christian point of view: no mercy is given to the characters of those, who will not listen to the Message; they are classed as idiots, profligates, obstinate atheists, fanatical Mahometans, debased Polytheists. I once read a Persian account of a war in Upper India, describing the dead on one side (the writer's side) as "all going to heaven," and the dead on the other as "going to hell": so in Missionary Reports, all, who become Christian, are angels, pure from sin, free from vice. This gives an absence of reality to a Human story, and does infinite mischief to the Great Cause. There is indeed an amount of Good in all. No one can have lived for years amid Hindu and Mahometans without respecting their practical excellences, and regretting their Religious errors. No one can have read the Veda and Korán without a recurrence of the same feeling, which came over him, when he read the Dialogues of Plato, viz , that the influence of God's Spirit was not entirely absent from good and holy men in all ages and climes. And no one, who has considered the practices of the nominal Christian, his gross Immorality, his utter contempt of Divine ordinances, his godless life, his unrepentant Death, his recklessness of the lives and welfare of inferior and weaker races, without feeling, that whatever may be the high standard of the Christian Conception, it has in the Nineteenth century entirely failed, practically as regards the masses, either to bring them to Christ, or to live lives of Morality.

I quote the words of a Bishop at the Nottingham-Church-Congress, on "Religious Indifference":

"The Bishop referred to the increasing Religious indifference " amongst those 'who are to be found in all our churches, who are " not communicants, and never exhibit any interest in vital " religion.' The size and rapid growth of the school of indifference " was one of the most dangerous signs of the times at the close of " the Nineteenth century. The multitude, who belong to this " school, are not open opponents of the Faith of Christ's cause; " but they simply sit still, and do nothing for Religion at home or " abroad. Ask any clergyman, who works his parish, and visits his " people, and knows their characters, which is the chief difficulty

"he has to contend with. I am certain he would tell you, that it
"is neither Romanism, nor extreme Ritualism, nor Erastianism,
"nor Broad-Churchism, nor systematic scepticism, nor any other
"'ism,' but a half-dead, torpid, indifference about any sort or kind
"of Religion."

The Bishop closed his address with the sorrowful remark: "'If
"open sin, and dissipation, and drunkenness, and love of the world,
"are ruining thousands of Churchmen, I am sure that utter in-
"difference about Religion is ruining tens of thousands.' Was
"there no remedy for that state of things? Could nothing be
"done to check the progress of Religious indifference, and restore
"health to our Sion? Nothing, in his opinion, could do it but an
"outpouring of the Holy Spirit. For that let them all pray, and
"besiege the Throne of Grace continually. The early Christians
"of the first six centuries turned the World upside down; yet they
"had none of our many advantages. They had, however, that which
"we seem to lack in 1897, the real presence of the Holy Spirit in
"their work, their preaching, their characters, and their lives.
"This was the secret of their power. This was what they wanted
"amongst them at the end of the Nineteenth century, more prayer,
"closer union with Christ, more of the real presence of God the
"Holy Ghost. For that Presence, when they left the Conference,
"let them resolve to pray, and never to cease praying."

And there is another painful feature, which has disfigured all Religious Conceptions in all periods of the History of the World, viz., the degradation arising from Priestcraft, and Interference of Worldly Rulers for their own political purposes. Take Christianity in the last Nineteen centuries, as it is more widely known, and consider how different is the present form, which it assumes, from the Teaching in Judaea. Consider the blemishes and the causes:

 I. The survivals of Paganism and Judaism.
 II. Wicked and Cruel Intolerance.
 III. Spirituality lost in the outward form of Ritualism.
 IV. Anthropomorphism: not only in the words but in the spirit.
 V. Dense formality.
 VI. Entire inability to keep the majority of mankind moral and holy.
 VII. State-Interference for passing worldly motives.
 VIII. Money-seeking, dignity-seeking, Priestcraft.
 IX. Scriptures denied to the Laity, or read in unintelligible Languages.
 X. Entire unreality of Worship in State-ceremonials, so-called Religions.
 XI. Sensational misinterpretation, and misquotation, of Scripture.
 XII. Dogmatism of an intolerable character on a subject not susceptible of legal proof, and resting entirely on Faith.

Symbolism appears to have been always the extreme weakness of the Christian Conception, and is so to this day. Why cannot God be worshipped, and prayer offered, in the same straightforward and truthful way, in which other Human affairs are conducted? What merit, or charm, is there in forms, and ceremonies, words which have lost their meaning, antiquated observances, and obsolete customs? Is there not a danger in these of formal surface-worship?

After a study of the tenets of all dead, or existing, Religious Conceptions of the World, and stretching out my hands across the abyss of centuries to the men of ancient days, who had Spiritual power given them to speak and write, and whose utterances have come down to us, to Zoroaster, Confucius, the Hindu Sages, Buddha, Socrates, Plato, and the writers of the Old and New Testament, whose breathing of blessed thoughts, clothed in immortal words, ring in our ears in the day, and dwell in our thoughts at night, the Soul seems to see, that God has been immanent in all the ages, and in all climes; dimly seen, imperfectly understood, in the form of Triads, or Avatáras (God born in the form of man). The Holy Spirit was dimly shadowed in the Paramátma, until, in the fulness of time, all was made clear by the Incarnation of the Son of God, and the new Dispensation to all Mankind; and I humbly submit that man, by much seeking, can hardly find a way of Salvation more simple, more complete, more universal, than what was preached in Judaea in Anno Domini, viz. :

I. Guilt of all mankind, with no single exception.
II. Repentance possible to all, without exception.
III. Faith in One powerful to save.
IV. Pardon through the Mediation of the Son of God.
V. Peace, as the result of Pardon, in this World and the next.
VI. Holiness through His Holy Spirit, without which no man can see God the Father.

Yet these precious Truths were not made known to the wise of that period, the Hebrews of Alexandria, the Greeks of Athens, trained in the Schools of Plato, the thoughtful men of Rome, such as Juvenal, Séneca, Epictétus, and Marcus Aurelius, but to a rural Asiatic population in dense ignorance, and a bigoted Priesthood, who laid stress on Sabbath-observances, eating with unwashed hands, giving tithes on every trifle, amputating the male body, men sunk in an intellectual state lower and more dangerous than that of their own ignorant peasantry. It was so ordained, and we can say no more, and by the time, that it became current in Europe, the Divine Truth had become again incapsuled, and again concealed in new veils of Human Ritual Superstitions, partly Judaic, and partly Pagan.

Let us now turn to the Future. I contributed to the International Oriental Congress held at Paris this year (1897) an Essay on the Modern Religious Conceptions, which have come into existence since the great Anno Domini, and which are therefore openly avowed enemies of the Christian Conception. This Essay is reprinted in my "Linguistic and Oriental Essays," Series V, in the English Language at p. 475, and in the French Language at p. 827. There are two Categories:

    I. The old Conceptions purified and adapted to the environment of a Civilized Society.
    II. Modern Conceptions formed from the blending of the old Conceptions with the Christian Conception, either consciously or unconsciously.

The first Category comprises:

    A. Neo-Judaism.
    B. Neo-Hinduism.
    C. Neo-Zoroastrianism.
    D. Neo-Buddhism.
    E. Neo-Confucianism.

The second Category comprises:

    A. Islam, with its latest evolution, Bábíism.
    B. Brahmoism.
    C. Theosophy.
    D. Hau Hau, etc., of New Zealand.
    E. Mormonism.
    F. Positivism or Comteism, or the Religion of Humanity.
    G. Agnosticism.
    H. Unitarianism.
    I. Theism.

The study of these new Spiritual Phenomena is one of deep interest. Morality of the highest stamp is professed by all: so far the World has advanced. At any rate those, who pass into any one of these new forms, know what they are doing: what they are abandoning, and what they are adopting. They are deliberating upon a matter of paramount importance to their Souls; they are making an election; they are secure of entire Tolerance. Some of them are desirous to propagate their views: they are bound by no ties of race, or Nationality. No one can say what the Future has in store.

In these days it is fairly argued whether,

    (1) The same Religious Conception was suitable to all periods of the existence of the Human race, the earliest as well as the latest.

(2) Whether in these last days the same Religious Conception is uniquely suitable to the scattered races of Mankind, in all their varying circumstances of climate, and environment, in all their stages of Culture.

As to the first point, I submit that a judgment cannot be pronounced: we have the great fact, that the Message was never communicated to Man before Anno Domini. As to the second, Experience seems to teach us, that the Doctrines taught in Judaea, free from the contamination of the Middle Ages, and Europe, are suitable to the Human race in every stage of Culture, under any possible environment, and that no other Conception so suitable has been suggested by the wit of man.

But the end is not yet: one only Kingdom, the British Empire, includes three hundred and fifty millions of population. An American periodical has this year brought out the facts strikingly. I quote it:

"On a vast plain, the 350,000,000 subjects of Queen Victoria are assembled before her throne, and on a table near the throne are the five Sacred Books of the East: the Bible, the Veda, the Korán, the Tripítaka, and the Zend-Avesta. Rising from her throne, the Queen says: 'Let all those, who believe in the divine inspiration of the Veda, take their sacred books and pass out and away,' and 200,000,000 go out, while but 150,000,000 remain. Sadly the Christian Queen again speaks: 'Let those, who believe in the Korán, now leave.' Her grief increases, as 60,000,000 more go out, and but 90,000,000 remain. Again she speaks, and again there is an exodus of those, who believe in the Tripítaka, the sacred book of the Buddhists, and in the Zend-Avesta of the Parsi, 40,000,000 more. Out of 350,000,000, only 50,000,000 remain, who accept the Scriptures of the Old and New Testaments, and only a part of these are heart-believers. This parable shows, that the disciples of Jesus still have much to do before it can be said, that the glad tidings have adequately been made known to every creature.—*The Advance*." ("Missionary Review of all the World," Boston, 1897.)

It has been wisely remarked (Max Müller, "Science of Mythology"), that the Human mind passed through four spheres of activity, from the earliest period within the reach of Knowledge, to the present day:

 I. Language: there is nothing more ancient.
 II. Myths: the first attempts at translating the phenomena of Nature and Thought.
 III. Religion, or the recognition of Moral Power, and in the end of *one* Moral Power behind and above all Nature.
 IV. Philosophy, or an exercise of the power of reason and thought, based on the data of experience.

Another thought presses on the mind, "the Silence of God," since the appearance in Human Form of His Son. In the elder centuries before the great Anno Domini, He was reported in the Legends of all the Ancient Religions, to be always speaking, and making Himself manifest as a seen and evident Agent in the affairs of men, each race thinking that they only were the object of His care. Thus grew into existence the Paraphernalia of the Ancient Conceptions, Theophanies, Visions of Angels, Miracles, Auguries, Dreams, Prophecy, Signs from Heaven, Divine Voices. In the latter part of the First century A.D., they ceased, ceased absolutely: the Fortune-teller, the Thaumatourgos, the beholder of Visions, are laughed at. We feel insensibly, that we are in a new Dispensation, and that the great God does not interfere directly, or indirectly, in Human affairs. We know not why unexplainable events happen: perhaps we may know hereafter, but each one of us at the close of his life, if a long one, knows, whether it has been Sunshine or Shade, that his affairs have been managed by an unseen Power in the best and wisest way possible.

Happy are those, who have found a resting-place in One, whom they can trust, the result of meditation, not of conventional acceptance. But we must not think arrogantly or hardly, or superciliously, of others: they are feeling after God, if haply they could find Him. The Neo-Judaist, the Brahmo-Somájist, the Bábí, the Comteist, the Unitarian, the Theist, are deserving of the highest respect, as far as we can judge from the utterances of their great and holy leaders. They are advancing, and understand the great Problem, but have not, according to our views, and their own admission, reached the Solution. They are Progressive in the right direction: leave them an open field. The Neo-Hindu, the Neo-Zoroastrianist or Parsi, the Neo-Confucianist, still appear to be unable to come out of their old bondage: the Neo-Buddhist, the Mahometan, the Agnostic, deserve that sympathy, which can hardly be extended to the Theosophist, the Hau-Hauist, and the Mormon, who are distinctly retrograde in the path of Spirituality.

Still, the state of the Human race spiritually seems to be more hopeful than it was in the centuries preceding the great Anno Domini, and the dark period of Romish Supremacy, something worse than Judaism and Paganism. "*Corruptio optimi pessima.*"

Section 2.

" The unconquerable desire, and manifest duty, of those, who
" *really* believe in a Religious Conception, to extend it to other
" races, and the whole of mankind, by peaceful argument, unselfish
" sacrifice, and inducements, wholly free from worldly advantages,
" and the Arm of the Flesh."

(1) Exordium.
(2) First period, up to 400 A.D.
(3) Second Period, up to the Reformation.
(4) Third Period, up to the end of the Eighteenth century.
(5) Conclusion.

All Historical details with regard to the Conversion of each country of Europe are omitted: they are fully stated by competent authors: my motive at present is to draw attention to:

(1) The continuity of the enterprise.
(2) The spirit, in which the work of Evangelization was attempted.
(3) The Methods employed.
(4) The good and bad features of these Methods.
(5) The totally different circumstances of the present Epoch.
(6) The lessons and warnings to be gained from the consideration of the terrible errors of the Past.

(1) *Exordium.*

One object is, to show that, under the impulse once given and the Command, there has been during the last eighteen and half centuries a movement, varying in speed at different times, sometimes indeed stagnant like a glacier, that is impeded, sometimes flowing like a stream, sometimes percolating under the soil. The story of the Conversion of Europe is not one, that reflects credit on the Human race: the Methods made use of were most erroneous, and foreign to the principles of Christianity: the intolerance, and wickedness, of some of the Evangelizers exceeded in atrocity anything attributed to the followers of Mahomet. The doctrines of Christ were not presented to the Non-Christian World in a Christian spirit, mainly on their own merits, unassisted by the Arm of the Flesh, or the influence of Power, or Worldly Temptation.

Another object has been to show, that the real Method of Evangelization is by,

(1) Preaching and teaching in the Vernacular of each country.
(2) Translating the Bible, and circulating it among the people.

There has been a continuity of this Method, though progressing at a different degree of speed, and in a more or less complete manner.

I do not describe work done, or praise, or blame, but show coldly what has been the Method, although grievously disfigured by the admixture of bad ingredients, and point out, that the stream of Evangelization now flowing at high tide, has sometimes sunk so low, because unholy Methods were used, and holy ones abandoned. Dr. Maclear well says : " The force of Missionary enthusiasm was " not quenched; its ardour was not extinguished : it may have " been overlain with worldliness and fanaticism, *but it existed* : " the line of contact was not broken ; the succession of the heralds " of the Cross was maintained." (Ely Sermon, p. 11.)

Just about the time when the Hebrew, after his return from Babylon, had discovered, or seemed to have dreamed of, the universal suitability of the Religious Conception entrusted to him for all mankind, the several National forms of Worship of the adjacent Nations, West of the Euphrates, shrunk into nothingness: their notions, suitable to the infancy of mankind, could not stand before the scorching light of the Schools of Philosophy : they disappeared, while the several Conceptions of the Nations East of the River Euphrates, not being exposed to the same Rationalistic test, have survived to our time in undiminished strength as regards the Millions of their followers.

If we were not historically certain, that it is the same Christianity, which was taught by the Apostles, and which is now taught in Christendom, we should scarcely recognize the developments, as exhibited in England, Russia, Spain, and France, as having possibly sprang from the same germ in Palestine, so totally different is the whole of their externals from the Gospel delivered by Christ. It took 350 years to stifle the dying Paganism of Greece and Rome. Six hundred years more were required to bring to Christ the chief of the barbarian races, which had pressed into Europe, Kelt, Teuton, and Slav; but it took another 800 years before the work of Conversion of Asia, Africa, Oceania, and America, was undertaken in earnest. And this is scarcely stating the full truth, for, if Christendom had been newly established in Europe, it had been trodden out in Asia and North Africa. There seemed to be a retrograde movement, for, while the Christian Missionaries in a desultory manner were making a few converts in Europe, the Mahometans were converting thousands of Christians to their new Faith in West Asia, North Africa, Turkey, and Spain. This, indeed, is an awful phenomenon for Christians to reflect upon.

It must not be supposed, that the Idea of propagating a new Religion was a new one: it is true, that all the Religions of the old world were National, and it was an understood thing, that each Nation had its established Religious Conception, and neither was able, nor desired to be able, to bring others to their view. Imperial Rome was content to tolerate all Rituals and Dogmas, so long as the Roman Religious Conception was respected. The ancient Hindu Sovereigns acted in very much the same way. However, five hundred years before Christ, Gautama Buddha had sent out emissaries to disseminate his peculiar Ideas, and form new Associations. People were willing to listen to them, and be converted, although no hope of a Future Life, or worldly advantage, was promised to adherents. The "Noble Way" of Buddha was Universal, for all mankind, and in that respect it differed from all other previous Religious Conceptions, which were strictly National. But, on the other hand, it was only for this World: there was no principle of a new Life both here and hereafter, such as was conveyed in the unique Conception of Repentance, Faith, Pardon, Peace, Holiness, through the Mediation of the Crucified and Risen Christ. It was the Conception itself, not the Idea of Universal Propagation of that Conception, which was the novel feature of Christianity.

"Slow was the rate of progress of the Conversion of Europe;
"there never was a period, when the flood was not really rising,
"though a casual glance would not detect it. In the darkest hours
"there was ever some streak of light: it is not God's Method of
"Rule to give at once great results." (Maclear's "Gradual Conversion of Europe," p. 12.)

I quote another thoughtful passage:
"But it is indeed an idle speculation to consider, what would or
"would not have happened, had God ordered the World's History
"otherwise than He has done. One weighty utterance is sufficient
"for us: '*When the fulness of time was come*, God sent forth His
"Son.' If, therefore, the World required preparation for that
"cardinal turning-point, if a certain condition of ripeness was
"required for the proper acceptance of the Gospel by man, then
"the History, which I have written in this volume, is probably
"a most vital and important step in that preparation, perhaps
"hardly less important than the Law, 'which was our schoolmaster
"to bring us unto Christ.' For that Law affected only the chosen
"people, whereas Hellenic culture affected the world." (Mahaffy's
"Greek Civilization.")

As regards Translation of the Scriptures, only twenty-one versions existed before the Reformation: there were about half a dozen weak attempts at other Languages, which came to nothing, but indicated the spirit of the time: with the exception of two or three very dark centuries, the work of Translation has never been suspended for more than a hundred years together, and then only by the interference of the Arm of the Flesh. In almost every period of the long succession of years from the Ascension to the present century, there has always been a special χάρισμα, not coming from the laying on of hands, but falling upon heart, intellect, brain, and hand, of some chosen servant to transfer the Scriptures from Language to Language, for the saving of Souls.

One feature characterizes the Biography of all great Missionaries: they were great students of the Scriptures, necessarily in the Latin Vulgate, as for one thousand years no other was available; but in Museums are exhibited interlineal glosses in the Vernacular, such as the Irish Glosses at Bobbio, and St. Gall, and the Anglo-Saxon in Great Britain, showing that some worthy men were not content with the mere melodious sound of the chanted Latin, but were desirous, that the new story should be understood by their people in their Mother-tongue. We have a singular illustration of this. Boniface stopped for the night at a monastery near Treves. A promising boy, aged 15, named Gregory, after the blessing given at supper, began to read aloud out of the Latin Vulgate. When he had finished Boniface remarked: "You read well and clearly: do you understand the meaning of the words?" The boy said, that he was quite sure that he did, and read the Latin over again. Boniface said: "I want you to tell me in German what you have just read in Latin": the boy admitted, that he could not do so. Boniface then translated it word by word, and preached on the subject: it made such an impression upon Gregory, that he left all and followed Boniface, to learn from him how to understand the Holy Scriptures. Later on the time of Monks was wasted in idle processions, and liturgical chants, and the meaning of Scripture clean forgotten.

(2) *First Period, up to* 400 A.D.

By the Edict of Milan the Christian Religious Conception became a "*Religio licita.*" This does not at the present Epoch seem a great favour to grant, but the same intolerant cries have at all times come up from an ignorant populace, backed by an interested Priesthood, who lived by the old Ritual. Let us consider for a moment how wonderfully the sense of Justice has developed, since 313 A.D. I have been stationed at Banáras in North India, a city full of Temples of the Hindu, and Mosques of the Mahometan. By the Laws of British India there is absolute Tolerance, so long as the necessary Police-Regulations are observed, and the Sixth Commandment is not broken, which forbids Murder under any possible pretence. "Αἶρε τοὺς ἀθέους," was the cry of the Roman populace in the time of the Emperor Marcus Aurelius. There was at that time no outward show of Temples, Statues, Processions, and Ritual, for the new Faith started on the principle that "God was a Spirit, to be worshipped in Spirit and in Truth"; and the absence of outward show gave the appearance of Atheism. When Protestantism arose against the Paganism of the Church of Rome, the same charge was brought against the so-called Heretics, that they were Atheists.

Blameable as was the policy of that great and wise Emperor Marcus Aurelius in ordering the New Religious Conception to be opposed, how much worse was the conduct of Theodosius in the destruction of the Temple of Serápis at Alexandria! How frightfully wicked was the conduct of the Christians of that period! Some of them had undergone persecution in their youth from the Pagan Romans, and yet in their old age they were active in persecuting the Pagans, and destroying their Temples. They were the legitimate ancestors of Torquemáda and the Inquisition.

The Emperor Julian has always been unjustly spoken of: he was disgusted by the servile conduct of the Christian Clergy; he had been educated at Athens, and was acquainted with some of the most celebrated Bishops, who had been taught there. In the life of Basil (I, 285) we have the famous letters which passed between him and Julian on the subject of some document. Julian wrote:

"'Ανέγνων, ἔγνων, κατέγνων."

Reply of Basil:

"'Ανέγνως, οὐκ ἔγνως εἰ γάρ ἔγνως, οὐκᾶν κατέγνως."

("Thou hast read, but not understood: for if thou hadst understood, thou would not have condemned.")

Julian is called the "Apostate." He was not more so than Constantine, or any other person, who changes his Religion. A Hindu who becomes a Christian is called so in India. At least Julian was tolerant. If he made an attempt to reintroduce Paganism, it was not the old Paganism of the degraded Roman Empire, but, as he was a thoughtful Philosopher of the School of Athens, he desired to reintroduce the Worship of the Great Gods of Greece and Rome with something of the reality of Christian Worship, and the purity of Christian life. The great figure of Jesus of Nazareth, the Son of God, did not in those days stand forth so conspicuously as it does now.

With the death of Julian, Paganism died as a ruling Power: it was not a compact body of Doctrine: it had no Sacred Books, but it had become a kind of *illuvies* of all the dying Theogonies of the Elder World. In the tombs of the Roman Legion, buried under the Roman wall of Northumberland, are found Inscriptions to Isis, Bona Dea, the Great Mother, etc., but they were all impregnated with the dry-rot of Philosophy, Agnosticism, and Atheism. Let not the Christian Religion fall to that state. Still, Literature remained in the hands of the Pagans in the Schools of Athens and Alexandria. It never occurred to the Roman Emperor to found purely Secular Institutions. The rural population (Pagani) clung to their local Shrines, their hereditary Religious ideas : they still climbed the mountain, or worshipped at the fountain ; the mother still called Lucina to her throes; the dying man still sacrificed the cock to Aesculapius. They attributed the dreadful calamities of Rome to their own neglect of the Ancient gods, who had made Rome what it was, but who had now departed and left the city to its fate. If the Emperors called themselves Christians, some of them were still as cruel and vicious as Nero : if the Priests were Christians, they had introduced intolerance, and allowed no Religious Conception to exist but their own.

The nominal Christians used to bring sheep, oxen, and pigs, to sacrifice at the altar of the new Saint, just as they had done before at the altar of the deposed god : they remained Pagans in heart though not in name. They were convinced, that their Saint could do what they wanted, *if he chose.* There was a sort of contract in their minds between the God of the Christians and the Saint to take care of the individual Worshipper, and they had reason to be angry if the Saint took the offerings, and did not grant the favour asked. They had not got further than the Patriarch Jacob in their view of the great Controller (Genesis, xxviii, 20-2) : "*Do ut des.*" If the Saint did not grant what they wished, they abused him, ill-used him, and beat him. The Human race is more true to its own grovelling, selfish, self, than is generally supposed ; and in their gross, carnal hearts, the same sentiments survive the change of form of Ritual or Dogma, and exist among so-called Christians to this day.

Augustine of Hippo remarked, that the Idols, driven from the Temple, still dwelt in the heart :

" Magis remanescent in cordibus idola quam in locis templorum."

They could not find it in themselves to think ill of what their Ancestors had done for so many centuries without suffering any bad consequences, and what they themselves had done in innocent childhood : the Past, the Glorious Past, of Rome weighed on them. Their idea of Tolerance was to crave it, when conquered, and to deny it, when in power. It was as difficult in the Roman Empire, as in British India, to wean an ignorant herd in a low state of Culture from Pagan Worship : they were never converted in the heart, and they adapted the old Temple, old Ritual, old phraseology, to the new Religious Conceptions, forced upon the base populace by official influence, and which was more suitable to the advance of the age. Development is of the very essence of the Religious Conception of the poor foolish Human race. Great Pan was clearly dead: Nature-Worship had passed away. The gods of Rome no longer satisfied the aspirations, the lazy desires of a *canaille*, which must have some place to resort to, and acknowledge some Power, or Personality, greater than themselves, to whom they could appeal.

We can here appreciate the exceedingly great value of the Protestant theories of Religion, which place the Conversion of the individual by peaceful and holy argument in the front, and we cannot value too highly that great Christian Free-Thinking Element, which guarantees the existence of Religious Liberty, Entire Tolerance, and Absolute Equality.

Bishop Lightfoot, in his Sermons on Christianity and Paganism (p. 66, 1890), writes:

"The source of the superiority of Christianity over Paganism "was fourfold:

"(1) A more enlightened faith in the will of the Unseen.
"(2) A heartier devotion to the cause of Humanity.
"(3) A more reverential awe for the Majesty of Purity.
"(4) A greater readiness to Do and Suffer."

A Neo-Platonist and a Mahometan would dispute this superiority: a Buddhist would claim, as his own, all these characteristics. The Bishop says at p. 80:

"Though Constantine, and his son Constantius, reigned 55 years, "Paganism was by no means disestablished; Christianity was "only tolerated. Both Emperors were only baptized *in articulo* "*mortis*: both were called Supreme Pontiff of the Heathen Cult, "which was still the Official Religion: both dead Emperors were "added to the Divinities of the Pantheon; coins place this fact "beyond doubt."

Then came Julian, A.D. 361, who tried to restore the old Religious Conception, but with a reformed Cult. Gratian, in A.D. 383, refused to be Supreme Pontiff, and Paganism was disestablished, and disendowed. The Temple of Serápis at Alexandria was destroyed A.D. 391. With the fall of the Empire Paganism perished outwardly, though still kept up in secret. Augustine's "City of God" reads like a Paean of triumph over its fall.

If the chance of war left British India at the mercy of a Hindu, or Mahometan, Potentate, it is possible, and probable, that they would, each in their own way, do something to restore the dignity and wealth of their ancient Religious Conceptions, but it would be found in practice, that the Neo-Hinduism, and Neo-Mahometanism, would be something essentially different from the old forms, for new ideas have been absorbed into the old body. Education, and contact with other Nations, and the general softening influences of Civilization, have done their work. Christianity would not be expelled, and its influences would still be felt. The Tolerance of the British Rule in India for more than a century has left its indelible mark on the character of the population.

Besides, there is a Development of the Religious idea always going on, though with different degrees of force with Nations on the different rounds of Human progress. "Two thousand years ago " there loomed through the mists of earlier Greek Thought the " consciousness of One God: it came with the sense of the Unity " of the World; it came with the sense of the Order of the World." (Hatch: Bampton Lectures, p. 173.)

Plutarch writes ("De Iside et Osire," p. 378): "There are not " different gods among different people, nor foreign gods, nor " Greek gods, nor gods of the South and North, but just as Sun, " Moon, and Sky, Earth and Sea, are common to all mankind, but " have different names among different races, so, though there be " one 'Reason,' who orders these things, and one 'Providence' " who administers them, there are different honours and appella- " tions among different races, and men use consecrated symbols, " some of them obscure, and some more clear, in this way leading " their thoughts on the path to the Divine. But it is not without " risk, for some men, wholly missing their foothold, have slipped " into Superstition, and others, avoiding Superstition, have fallen " into Atheism."

How Missionaries should ponder over these lines! The idol is nothing, absolutely nothing: to exhibit it at Missionary Meetings, or even in a Museum, unless done reverently, is an insult to the Human race. The piece of wood or stone represents the Religious Conception of one of the poor uninstructed Children of God, " who felt after God if haply he could find Him." Both Hindu and Romanists have said to me, that it was not the image, which they venerated, but the idea personified in that image. By looking intently at the image, and for the moment forgetting all the World besides, they tried to fix their Souls upon the Infinite. Perhaps shutting their eyes would have the same result to Souls habitually living close to God.

It is not sufficiently dwelt upon, how in the 400 years preceding Anno Domini, the whole civilized World was entering on a new realm of thought: Confucius in China, Buddha in India, Socrates, and the School of Plato, in Greece, were leaving indelible marks on the minds of men. Great Pan was dying: an incurable wound had been inflicted on the old National Religions, by Reason and Ridicule: the Jews, even the most rigorous, were advancing, in spite of their Thora, along the same path. Civilization is as infectious as Cholera, and travels from town to town; and parties, susceptible of the intellectual and spiritual infection, are found everywhere.

In no one particular were the eyes of men more open than this: What is the reward of Virtue? what profit has man in keeping the

Law of God? The Hebrew before the Exile had no thought beyond this World; temporal blessings were the only reward, and yet clearly the good suffered, and the wicked triumphed. It is of no use for the Psalmist to say, that he never saw the righteous begging their bread (xxxvii, 25): facts were against him.

When the Hebrew Kingdom was entirely destroyed, and the Persian and Greek ruled, when Antiochus Epiphanes defiled the Temple, it then came upon them, that the reward was not in this World, and that there was a Future State. Homer and the Greeks had arrived at this earlier; the Latins knew all about the next World; the Hindu and Buddhist solved the problem by Metempsychosis.

The early death of Josiah was a crushing event. Of what use was it to serve God? The explanation in the Psalms of what was seen in the Temple did not cover the problem: the wisdom of the Son of Sirach is at fault to explain it.

Another point of view has to be considered. The elder World, including Greece and Rome, looked upon the State-Religion, the Local Deity, as part of the Constitution, part of the ethnical, local, and moral, prospects of the Nation, which could neither be questioned, nor changed. Plato and Cicero clearly admitted this fact. The man, who doubted, or left his National Faith, was declared to be "Impious," to have committed a crime against the State, and deserving of Punishment.

Christianity, following Buddhism, and preceding Mahometanism, introduced a new principle, that Religion was Universal, and not limited to this or that Nation. While the Christians were downtrodden, they pleaded for Tolerance on the ground of National Law, and that the Divinity required the service of the Heart. The Edict of Milan provided, that each person should be allowed to worship his own Deity, in order that that Deity might look favourably on the Empire. This admits the existence of other Deities, and proves, that the Edict could not have been drafted by a Christian, who could not make such an admission. The Hebrews may have been up to the time of the Prophets Monolatrists, and not Monotheists, admitting that Moab and Ammon had their gods, but that their God was a stronger one; but the Christian and the Mahometan were never so.

When the time came for the Teutons to give up the Worship of their Divinities, whose names still survive in the days of the week, the lower classes did little more than obey orders, and debase the New Religious Conception to the level of the old by changing the terminology, not the idea. With the usual ingratitude of Perverts, while the Priests of the new Conception took credit for the abundance of the Harvest, the cessation of illness, victory in battle in reply to their prayers, when opposite events occurred, they were attributed to the wrath of the insulted Teuton Gods. I have not remarked this intellectual phenomenon in India, for in fact the Worship of the old gods has not diminished, and the erection of new Temples, and repair of old ones, in a time of Peace, and a realm of Law, are conspicuous.

Of those, who opposed Christianity in the fourth century A.D., there were distinct groups:

(1) Those who would make no compromise: the stupid old conservatives, who exist at all periods, who know nothing, understand nothing, and remain in their ignorance.
(2) Those who, from a desire of a quiet life, kept silent.
(3) Those who, being moderate in their views, and thoughtful in their natures, dreamed of some union and compromise between the old and new Idea.

All the above were firmly attached to the old Religious Conception, as would be natural with persons of low Culture; but the worldly people, indifferent to anything spiritual, went over blindly to the new Religious Conception of those in Power. The greater the amount of Paganism, that clung to the new Ritual, the more staunch these adherents were: but the eyes of the generations of mankind were being opened to the folly of Polytheism, the frightful moral impurity of the Olympian gods, and a conviction grew upon the thoughtful, that there did exist a great Eternal Universal Power, known as Numen Divinum Divinitas, the author and sustainer of the World. We may expect something like this in the expiring Religious Conception of the Hindu and Buddhist.

The Biography of one man of that period of change has come down to us, which is characteristic of the Epoch. In the last generation of real Paganism there lived a man named Practextátus. He died 384 A.D., before Alaric appeared before Rome. He was a tolerant, wise, genuine, man, well skilled in all the learning of the time. He not only knew the history of his own Graeco-Roman Cult, but of the other contemporary Conceptions, such as those of Mitra, Isis, the Great Mother, etc., and he tried to unite them all, so as to resist lawfully and with dignity the new Christian idea. He was a contemporary of Jerome and Augustine.

When the Christians quarrelled among themselves, and actually killed each other in a dispute about the election of a new Pope, Practextátus interfered, exiled one of the candidates, and supported Dámasus. He gave Christians the cynical advice, that they should love each other more: he rallied them on their luxurious living, and large Revenues. The Inscription on the tomb of his wife Paulina has come down to us: " You, my husband, by teaching me have saved " me from the arm of Death : you took me to the Temple, and " under your eyes I was initiated into all the mysteries. I should "have been happy, if the gods had allowed me to survive you. I am still happy, because I die thine, as I lived, and as I shall still remain after my Death." This is coming very near Christianity. The moderate Christians and Pagans might have united: but just as in former times the Pagans had persecuted the Christians, so later on the Christians persecuted the Pagans, and so it would be again, if the Church of Rome, which learns nothing, and forgets nothing, got into power.

(3) *Second Period: Conversion of Europe.*

Many excellent Books have been written on this subject; they are all partizan-books. I wish to regard the progress of the new Idea from a philosophical point of view. If any enlightened Mahometan, like Saiyad Ahmed Ali, of Aligarh, North India, were to write a Book on the Conversion of Asia to Islam, and to narrate with satisfaction, how Christian Churches were destroyed or turned into Mosques, and the Priests slaughtered, and their lands confiscated, we should pass a severe judgment upon him. The end does not justify the means. We ought to recollect, that the Powers of the Earth are only instruments in the hands of the great Controller of Human events. We look with equal disgust on the Methods adopted in past ages to make Nations Christian, or to make them Mahometan.

Europe to this day is not entirely even nominally Christian: there are Millions of Mahometans in the European portion of the Turkish Empire, and thousands of Hebrews scattered over Europe. As a fact, portions of Lithuania were not converted to a Nominal Christianity until the Thirteenth century A.D., and then by the most violent and abominable Methods. Up to 1230 A.D., Human Sacrifices were offered in Lithuania, and male and female slaves were burned with their Master and Mistress. Moreover, Millions are only Census-Christians. The Unitarians can scarcely be classed as Christians for any practical purpose, any more than the Hebrew.

There was a marked difference in the mode of Conversion. In the early centuries the spread of the new Idea had gone upwards, springing sometimes from the words, and example, of a Christian slave, male or female. The first Christians were essentially men of low degree, not many wise, not many great, nor were the tenets of the new Idea formularized, nor were the Ministers instructed, nor was there any Literature of any kind. There must have been a very difficult two centuries, when the new Idea rested on its own innate strength, and Divine impulse.

The political state of Europe was changing. Powerful and ignorant Pagan races had spread over North Europe from the East, the Kelts, the Teutons, and the Slavs: they were the vehicles chosen by God for the reception of the new Idea from the worn-out Roman and Greek races. They were followed by the Huns. The Roman arms had penetrated to Britain in the North, that isolated race,

"*Penitus totâ divisos orbe Britannos*";

to the South in the African Sahára, to the East to the shores of the River Tigris and beyond. Greek Philosophy had shaken the blind confidence in the Supernatural. The common herd had not much of the Religious Instinct to get rid of, and they did not take in much beyond the externals of the new Religious Conception.

From one point of view the whole Christian community in the first two centuries had the functions to discharge of a Missionary Society, and had the opportunity also. They were strangers and sojourners in the midst of a great mass of Paganism: there was no standing still, or making compromise. They had not to go out of their street, or their town, to find persons worthy of Conversion: there were their slaves, their neighbours, their fellow-townsmen. The very words which they used, their every action, if they were indeed Christians, betrayed them. The Christian mistress could not ill-treat her slave; the Christian man could not give a free rein to his low appetites; the soft answer, the abstention from returning a blow, the putting up with injuries, betrayed a something, which made an impression, disarmed an enemy, and perhaps attracted an inquirer. The meeting for family-prayer, the Psalm-singing, the pure life of chastity, must have made Pagans feel, that there was some new element in life, that there was a Beauty in Holiness, a Power in self-control. Such exhibitions in the Nineteenth century would have the same effect. In Rome, at that time, the masses, who took lessons in Cruelty in the Flavian Amphitheatre, had lost all sensibility to Pity, all capacity for Mercy.

Of course, those, who opposed the spread of Christianity in the three first centuries, get no quarter from an Ecclesiastical Historian. Clearly, like the Hindu conservatives in India, they did not understand the movement: it was clearly a *destructive* one; of that there was no doubt, and destructive of something, which had been valued by them. They were good old conservatives, who were content with things as they were: the Olympian gods would last their time, and they had no stomach for martyrdom.

And it has been acutely remarked by a great author, Dr. Arnold, that in all great moral movements there are two motors, belonging to totally different classes: (1) the serious reformer, (2) the libertine anarchist. The Apostles had to warn their flocks against the wild licentious doctrines, which had fastened like limpets on an imperfect Christianity. The neo-Christian, both then and now, fell far short in practice of the doctrine, which he preached. Those, who persecuted Socrates, called him an Atheist: that was according to the prevailing opinion of the time. Those, who persecuted the Christians, called them Atheists; and, when the Christians got the upper hand, and the Arm of the Flesh was on their side, the Christians called the Heathen Atheists. It is the old story: orthodoxy means " my doxy," and atheism means the non-recognition of " my gods." We have to get to the standpoint of the speaker to understand the argument.

The problem of the Conversion of Europe seems to resemble the problem of the Conversion of India at the present moment: but how different is the environment! While, on the one hand, the preacher of the new Idea has entire Toleration, and liberty, so long as he does not injure others, and has no fear of incarceration by the Authorities, or of being stoned by the Mob in a Realm of Law, yet, on the other hand, he dares not touch, or insult, a place of Worship of others, and, if such an incident had occurred as that of the deaths of Ananias and Sapphira, while I was Magistrate of Banáras, I should have placed Peter and John in the Police Lock-up, and inquired into the cause of death. Had Hypátia been killed by the Bishop and Clergy of an Indian Diocese, I rather suspect, that the parties concerned, including the Bishop, would have found their way to the Gallows.

Whether by the connivance of the Christian Priests or not, somehow or other the converts in Europe, notably in Friesland, connected the abundance of the Harvest, and the success of the Fishery, with the arrival of the Christian Missionary: this is the very lowest form of Superstition. When will the enlightened Christianity of the Nineteenth century disconnect the solemn order of the Seasons, and the laws, which regulate the abundance and scarcity of the Seasons, from Prayer and Temple-Worship? In India to this day Prayers are being offered simultaneously in adjacent temples for more Rain, by those who have Cotton-cultivation, and for no Rain at all, by those, who cultivate the Sugar-cane on irrigated land. Why not leave the Clerk of the Weather to manage his own affairs?

So when, by use of medical knowledge, or some lucky chance, in fact by the Providence of God, and His all-seeing Wisdom, men recovered from sickness, the converts in the Early Missions in Europe were taught to attribute this healing to the new Religious Conception: how the Deaths were explained away we know not. But it is a low form of Conversion to retain such notions. Possibly such stories may belong to the lying legends of an over-credulous age. It must be admitted, that out of Palestine no consideration is shown by the most devout Christian to a Miracle. The modern Missionary should stoutly disclaim all sympathy with any Reports of occurrences out of the ordinary evolutions of Nature. The medicine-man, the Θαυματοῦργος, or the Faith-healer, should be sternly denounced. The spiritual Conversion of a Soul is the greatest possible Miracle. The saving of a Soul from well-merited Punishment by Faith in one Powerful to save is the greatest of all possible Human Conceptions.

Not only was it deemed to be right, but a duty, to compel the Heathen to come in to the Christian Church, and to punish severely any, who after joining the Church, altered their mind and left it; but this right is asserted still by no less an authority than Cardinal Vaughan: " Occasions are not wanting for the employment of the " Civil sword in defence of the Church. Neither the Church nor " the State, whenever they are united on the basis of Divine Right, " have any knowledge of Tolerance. The Peace of Christ goes " hand in hand with Unity, not with Division. The Church has " the right, *in virtue of her Divine Commission, to require of everyone* " *to accept her doctrine*: there can be no tolerance of error in " matters of Religion." (Cardinal Vaughan, " Essays on Religion," p. 402, 1867.)

The influence of a Queen was made use of to convert a King. We have the notable instance of the King of Kent in the time of Augustine of Canterbury. Great indignation would be felt, if a Mahometan wife persuaded a Christian King to accept Islam. A whole Regiment of Soldiers entered the stream *en masse* to be baptized under orders of their Chieftain. Three thousand French warriors were baptized then and there with King Clovis. The Russian peasants were driven by whips into the River Dnieper, and baptized by force. They would have become Mahometans under similar influences brought to bear upon their bodies. Cases of individual Conversion under the influence of argument and prayer were rare.

In those days there was not such a wide abyss of social habits between the Missionary and the Natives, to the Conversion of whom he was delegated, as there exists now. The hardship, to which the Missionary was exposed from climate and entire deprivation of social necessities, was much less. As a set-off to this, in a Realm of Law like British India there is no personal danger from arbitrary violence, and unfailing means of communication with the mother-country, which were entirely wanting in the days of the great English Missionary Boniface.

Alcuin (A.D. 780) insisted on the worthlessness of Baptism without Faith and conviction of Sin. He did not regard Baptism as an *opus operatum*, and he did not scruple to inveigh against the tendency at his time to identify Conquest by force of arms with the Conversion of the Soul. We stretch out our arms to bless this mediaeval Christian, who could see and speak so clearly.

Let us read what happens in our own Epoch. A thousand of the troops of the newly converted King of Kent and his French wife had indeed walked into the River and were baptized: not a word about Soul-Conversion. In modern times Tippu Tib, the great Slave-dealer, sells to the emissaries of Cardinal Lavigerie, a complete village of slaves captured with the usual accompaniments of rapine, rape, murder, and arson, men, women, and children, in the proper proportion, and all are baptized and started in a Christian Church: what an outcry there would be, if the Mahometans had done the same, and had circumcised Christian Boys!

The Bishop at Loanda used to baptize all the slaves forcibly deported for the Portuguese West African Colony from South America.

There was an ebb and flow in the tide of Missionary zeal. Gregory the Great seriously and justly blamed the French Churches, which had obtained an early Christianity, for not caring to carry the Gospel to their Pagan Neighbours. The same slackness was evidenced by the British Church, which actually refused to take any steps to convert the Anglo-Saxon invaders of Britain. Somehow or other the Pagan Northmen, who had settled in North France, reappear to History as Christian Normans.

Still more remarkable is the absence of any desire of the great Protestant Reformers of Europe, though they had studied the Scriptures and were devoted to Christ, to carry the Gospel to Regions Beyond. Even in the reign of Queen Elizabeth no effort was made. It cannot be said, that at that Epoch the Duty was unknown, as Erasmus, not a Protestant, but whose voice was heard in his Missionary treatise, pp. 115, 116, recognizes the Duty.

Boniface's Methods were thoroughly bad, exceptionally bad from the standpoint of his own Epoch. He used the Arm of the Flesh unscrupulously to overcome the inhabitants of another country (he was an Englishman and the people were Germans), who had different views from his own of the relation of the Soul to God. He might by kindly reason and argument have shown them the better way: but where was his authority in the Scriptures to destroy their objects of reverence, appropriate their property to his own use, and while getting rid of Idol-Worship with one hand, introduce the still more degraded fetish-Worship of relics with the other? He erred greatly in another direction. He strove by force or chicanery to force into obedience to Rome the independent Christianities founded on the Continent by Columbánus and Gall: he is reported to have baptized thousands: how many individuals had he tested as to their knowledge, elementary knowledge, of Christ? He was not a hypocrite: he never pretended to work miracles: he wrought according to the limitation of Human powers, with an inflexible will and entire devotion to Rome and the Frank King, who supported him.

Charlemagne attempted to introduce Christianity by blood and sword into Germany; he beheaded in one day 4,500 Saxons, who opposed him. One of the main causes of the irruption of the Northmen upon Great Britain, Ireland, and France was to avenge the wrong done by Charlemagne. (Stoke's "Keltic Church," p. 264.) He did not scruple to destroy idols, and appropriate the Temples to the new Idea: a greater wrong than this to Human Nature can scarcely be imagined. Cardinal Vaughan, in his address this year (1897), seems to allude to this with satisfaction at the Ebb's Fleet celebration. The Pope ordered that the Temples of the idols were not to be destroyed, but sprinkled with holy water, and furnished with altars, on which Worship could be offered to deified mortals, such as the Virgin Mary.

Still, the Missionaries of that period were devoted men, and did what they could: there were no "Missionary Intelligencers" published monthly to cover them with undeserved praise, and chronicle the illnesses of their wives, and the prolific birth of their children. Their names have become mere shadows. We have the outlines of good and devoted men, who made it their life's occupation in a rude and barbarous age, with no support from rich Associations, no Salaries, or Pensions, or Allowances, no motive but to serve their Master, no instructions but the promptings of the Holy Spirit to spread the gentle civilizing precepts of the new Religious Conception.

If not of the same race with the men, amidst whom they settled, they were on the same round of Human Culture, in the same environment of customs and prejudices, and under the same cloud of ignorance as to Geography, History, and Astronomy. There was no superb Albocracy then as now, and they dealt tenderly with the usages of the people, as they could sympathize with them, pitied their superstitions, from which they had so lately emerged themselves, and if permitted became fathers of their new flock. Boniface started from Exeter, Columbanus from Glasgow, Aidan migrated to the Holy Island: let us think of their material outfit, and contrast it with that of the modern Missionary, who is outfitted by a Missionary Society. Let us reflect on the comfortable homes of the modern Missionary, his carriages, and the dress of himself and his wife, and how he holds his head above the Native Pastors, and would scorn the idea of his daughter's intermarriage with one of them: he rails against Caste, and in matters matrimonial and social practises it: perhaps the converted Hindu, like the late Nehemiah Nilkant, a Brahman, has a pedigree of hundreds of years; while the white man has sprung from behind the counter into the pulpit.

The Missionary of that period craved of the Ruler the gift of a petty island, or some valueless land, and practised Community life, as distinguished from Monasticism. In his humble way he exhibited the new Christian life, analogous to the "Noble Way" of Buddha, and he went about preaching the new Idea of Human Life, and the Promise of Life beyond the grave. Sometimes the Chiefs threw in their lot with him. In Iona the Abbot was head of the Community, and the Bishop was one of the Community. Such servants of Christ did not seek personal comfort: they did not allow themselves the blessings of Family-life: they were celibates, and their food, raiment, and rooftree, were of the same pattern as that of the people, whose hearts they came to win. They employed Natives as their assistants: they laid the foundation of Secular Instruction: they all spoke the Language of the People: they studied and translated the Scriptures, and with their own hand made copies for the new Churches. There were no Printing-presses then. Patrick, Columba, Columbanus, and Boniface, had all studied the Scriptures, and loved to read and meditate upon them, and made them their rule in life: if asceticism could be imputed to them, it was only external. "True Religion," said Columbanus, "consists not in the humiliation of the body, but of the heart: the external observances are not the end, but the means."

On the subject of the Language to be employed in Public Worship, Augustine of Canterbury was blind: he chose to assume, that Latin was the Sacred Language. Ulfilas, Cyril, Methodius, had their eyes opened: his were shut. Latin was dead, dead even in Spain and Italy, and had never been understood in Great Britain; but the Anglo-Saxon, and Welsh, Languages were entirely banished from the Churches, over which he had control, and no attempt was made to translate the Scriptures. The Priest kept to himself the prerogative of oral explanation. It was not so in North Britain, where the Missionaries from Iona had influence. Cædmon (A.D. 680) burst forth with a poetic Bible: this was followed by a Translation of the Psalms, and Bede left to us the precious legacy of the Gospel of John.

Twice this little island of Great Britain has had the privilege of being called to Evangelize the World. The names of Aidan, Paulinus, Chad, Cuthbert, Benedict Biscop, Wilfrid, Willebrod, Winefrid *alias* Boniface, can never be forgotten.

(4) *Third Period.*

The time came, when the Gospel was conveyed to countries out of Europe. The efforts, that have been made during the Nineteenth century by the Protestant and Romish Churches, are too well known to require mention. Allusion is now made to the efforts made on a very limited scale in previous centuries. We must recollect that locomotion then was difficult: Geographical Knowledge was scant and inaccurate. In Mahometan countries, both to the Missionary and Convert, change of Faith meant Death, and in barbarous Regions fearful sufferings had to be counted upon. We must not be hard on previous generations, because so little was done. It is true, that they did not even do what they might have done, but the magnificent opportunities of modern days were absent. Of course the same Duty existed; but the means were wofully deficient, and the Methods had not been worked out by experience. The countries, in which some efforts had been made, were:

I. Asia: India, China, Japan.
II. Africa: Abyssinia.
III. Oceania: nothing.
IV. America: Mexico, Paraguay.

The prospect of the same Gospel being preached in the same country (say British India) by twenty or thirty different Organizations, in differing forms, sometimes violently hostile to each other, is not encouraging: it is a melancholy phenomenon.

Foremost, but by no means the originator, among Missionaries of this Period stands Francis Xavier: he landed in Goa 1542 A.D., and died aged 46, 1552 A.D., after service of only ten years in Goa, Travancór, Ceylon, the Indian Archipelago, and Japan: he died of want and neglect in the little island of Sancian, near Hongkong. His Methods were decidedly sensational, and spasmodic. In the *Illustrated Catholic Missions of London*, Dec., 1890, in a short notice barely exceeding a column of half-page, it is deemed of importance to record, that at Goa he "went about the streets ringing a bell to draw the little children after him": in Ceylon he "evangelized the poor and oppressed" Pearl-fishers, "baptizing *tens of thousands*": in Travancór "God first gave him the gift of tongues without learning them." In describing his Methods the writer says, that his life was not merely that of a great "thaumaturgus," miracle-worker, "but first and foremost a life of self-denial, mortification, penance, "and humiliation, combined with heroic love of God, and conse- "quent zeal for souls; and wherever Missionary work has succeeded, "is succeeding, or will ever succeed, it is only by these Methods, the "Methods of the Apostles, Patrick, Boniface, Xavier, and all who "are animated by his spirit, and hope for his reward." Oh that the Missionaries of the Church of Rome would be content with these last attributes, omitting the thaumaturgy! Oh that the Protestant Missionaries would take up a life of self-denial, and be ready to die at their posts, not saddling the Missionary Society with the education of Missionary children, and abandoning their posts, just, when after a useless and expensive apprenticeship, they have become useful, for the sake of a sick wife! Can such be called Apostles?

Xavier's merits were: absence of Ambition, and Vanity; undaunted energy; entire self-consecration; no idea of leaving his Field; very bold; the same to all men; sympathy and tenderness for all his fellow-labourers; a peacemaker always; great nobility of character; very full in his reports; good for dispatch of business; great purity of life; great endurance and patience.

His faults were: leaning entirely on the Arm of the Flesh; ignorance of any foreign language; not truthful; impulsive and constantly meddling in Worldly Politics; revengeful against all, who opposed him; totally indifferent to the Translation of the Bible; worshipper of Saints and Angels; encouraging his Missionaries to flatter and act as spies; requiring no preparation before baptism; an ascetic; desirous to be an autocrat; crave for Romance; baptizing young children *in articulo mortis*; never making any attempt at individual Conversion of the Soul.

It was found, that in the South of India, in Travancór, there was an ancient Syrian Christian Church: the date of the foundation of that Church is disputed: it is not probable, that it existed before the Sixth century A.D., and there is little evidence of Christian life during ten centuries; but it did exist, and maintained a certain Ritual, ruled over by an Abúna from the Syrian Patriarch at Mardin, in Mesopotamia. Francis Xavier, in 1545, tried to induce a spiritual submission to the Pope by offering a salary to this Abúna from the Portuguese King: this is a sample of the Missionary Methods of the Period. Strange to say, the Syrian Church preferred its independence, but there was a secession of a portion, who called themselves the Syro-Romanists, under the Bishop of Goa. When they first came into contact with Western Christians, they were Nestorians, and had been so from the commencement; but in 1665, when all communication with the Nestorian Patriarch had long been effectually prevented by the Romanists, they came under the Patriarch of Antioch of the Syrian Church. ("Syrian Church of Malabar," 1873, p. 7.)

It is interesting to record, that a small section of the Romish Missionaries tried the expedient of a certain fusion of Romish and Indian practices, if not of dogma: it failed, as the Vatican rejected the notion with scorn. The Phenomenon is possible in the present dissolving state of the Indian Intellectual Kaleidoscope. The Salvation-Army supplies a quasi-Christian ingredient, which might combine with a branch of the great Hindu Tree.

This is one of the Problems of the Twentieth century. Missionary Societies of all Churches and Nationalities have, in spite of warning, persistently determined to convey to the inhabitants of Asia, Africa, Oceania, and North and South America, the Gospel of Christ in a European, or American, capsule, so that the converts not only become Christianized but Europeanized. There will be an intellectual revolt on the part of the ancient races of Asia: they were civilized, when the people of Europe were still savages. They have Legends, ancient Ritual, time-honoured Customs, Sacred Books, National Pride: will they not submit the precious ore of the Gospel to a new crucible, and refuse to occupy the position of Middle-class Europeans and Americans?

(5) *Conclusion.*

We must not suppose, that God's witnesses are at any time entirely absent from any great assembly of Human creatures. Amidst the Hindu, Buddhists, Confucianists, and Mahometans, there have at all times been some, who tried to see God face to face, or attain that spiritual state, which was closest to God, or partook of the elements of the highest Virtue conceivable by their limited intellects. So amidst those dark ages of Christianity, when Religion was being propagated by the sword, false miracles, lying legends, and unworthy expedients, amidst this wilderness of true Religious Conceptions, amidst these dry bones of Ritual observance, the cruel oppression of the poor non-Christian, the destruction of time-honoured shrines, which had been the only ideal of Religion to countless Millions for centuries, ever and anon we come upon the track of true Saints of God. Some sparks from the Divine Workshop illuminate the whole Region: wiser counsels are uttered, if not attended to: the faults above described were the faults of the Messenger, not of the Message. Something whispers in our ear, that the matter was from God, and not from Rome, or Gaul: that this was the Method deliberately ordained for the Conversion of Europe, for the object was to advance the Kingdom of God, not the transitory Kingdom of Roman, Kelt, Teuton, or Slav. The work was painfully Human; the workers poor miserable men; the object was essentially divine, *to convert the heart.* Some think, that this spiritual operation can be performed by Ritualistic Symbols, brought to bear *en bloc* on families, tribes, and Nations; others think on Scriptural grounds, that Conversion is the sole work of the Holy Spirit working on individual consciences. We sadly remark the absence of charity in what was done: let me take heed, that there is no lack of charity in the mode of describing it: the treasure is given to us in earthen vessels; but it is given, and it is there: let us condemn the fault, but speak lovingly of the offender. Perhaps, if we had been placed in their environment, we should have done the same: perhaps in Heaven the desire to do His Will will be some excuse for the shockingly defective modes of doing it.

A narrowness of vision is evidenced in many writers; their environment was practically limited by the Roman Empire, the orbit of Greek and Roman Literature with the conventional knowledge of the Hebrew race. The knowledge of Eastern Asia, Africa, Oceania, and America was limited, and yet the four great pre-Christian Religious Conceptions had come into existence, Brahma, Buddha, Zoroaster, Confucius, influencing hundreds of millions even to this day. The English theologian discusses the work of the Great

Creator over *the whole World*, the round orb circumnavigated by our ships, and described by our Geographers, and yet he restricts his arguments to the comparatively small Roman Empire, or the insignificant Hebrew race, as if they represented the whole World. Luke the Evangelist set the example by telling us that Augustus Caesar issued a decree "that all the World (ἡ οἰκουμένη) should be taxed," and that "devout men out of every Nation under Heaven" were present on the day of Pentecost (Acts, ii, 5). This has led insensibly in Religious treatises to the use of exaggerated and lax expressions, which would never be used in the description of the affairs of ordinary life. A kind of poetic glamour is thrown over the whole subject, and things are deemed to be possible, which are in ordinary life impossible. And yet the subject discussed is of such paramount importance to the Soul, that the strictest accuracy of expression should be maintained.

For Luke, the Gentile Physician, Buddha had lived in vain; for him in vain had Asóka two hundred years before the great Anno Domini erected the tablets, which still exist in different parts of the vast Indian Empire, preaching Peace, and Mercy, and Holiness. "A completely new idea in the History of
" the World had been started in the third Buddhistic Council
" in the Third century before the great Anno Domini under
" King Asóka, the idea of conquering all Nations by the sole
" Power of Truth. A resolution was carried at that Council to
" send Missionaries to all Nations to preach the Noble Way, the
" new Gospel of Altruism. Such an idea had never entered
" into the minds of the ancient Egyptian, Babylonian, or Brahman,
" or Hebrew, not even of the Greeks: it presupposed quite
" a new conception of the World; it assumed a belief, that the
" different Nations of the World, however separated from each
" other by language, colour, custom, and Geographical distribution,
" formed one united family; that Humanity was not an empty
" name." (Max Müller, Oriental Congress, September, 1892.)

We have no right to attribute Universality to the experiences of the tiny Nation of the Jews, or to claim a monopoly of moral goodness to the Nineteenth century nominal Christian. The great Asiatic Nations up to the time of Alexander the Great had maintained an isolated existence: they had neither borrowed ideas, nor lent them: they created, each of them, their own Philosophy, developed their own form of Ritual, and gave birth to their own gigantic Literature. Buddha first broke the silence and the isolation of past centuries: Buddhism, driven from Nearer India, took refuge in Further India, and the Extreme Orient.

The interference of the Civil Power with the work of the Missionary is quite legitimate, if his conduct be such, as is likely to cause a breach of the Peace, and loss of life. I myself in the Panjáb ordered the Chapel of a Missionary to be pulled down, which he had erected on the edge of a sacred tank, regardless of the feelings of the Hindu worshippers. The French Government in Algeria is always in anxiety, lest the unguarded words of the Missionary should rouse the indignation of the people, and cause political trouble. The only remedy is, to expel the Missionary, if he attempts to turn the world upside down. The Government of British India may be compelled to do so also, if the Missionary will continue to interfere with the Laws Regulating the Sale of Alcohol, the Opium-Trade, and the internal administration of Military Cantonments, forgetting the Lord's words : " Render unto Caesar the things, which are Caesar's, and unto God the things, that are God's."

The advantages and disadvantages of high European Civilization are pretty equally balanced. The European Missionary considers himself so socially superior to the Natives, that his influence for good is diminished. The Press, if a blessing on one side, is a cause of boundless evil on another: the power of locomotion, and the entire Toleration of all forms of Worship, are not without corresponding drawbacks.

We are gradually freeing ourselves from the notion, that the Nicene Fathers were inspired, or better informed, and wiser than those, who happened to be born centuries later: it is admitted now by Roman Catholic and Protestant, that our Lord's great Commission is binding on all, and that it has never been fulfilled.

What said the early Fathers ? Setting aside those, who adopted Millennium-ideas, it does not appear, that a universal reign of the Gospel was anticipated before the end of the World. Chrysostom considered, that the Prophecies of the preachers of the Gospel had been adequately fulfilled before the taking of Jerusalem. Jerome considered, that the whole of Isaiah xi had reference to the first advent of our Lord. Basil and Cyril entertained the same view ; they applied the Prophecies to the spread of the Gospel, that had been already witnessed. Augustine wrote on the signs of the approaching end : the Gospel was to be preached *for a witness* in all lands : that the accomplishment of this would be a sign of the coming end : the result of the Preaching would be, not that *all* would believe, but some only, and that the rest would be unbelievers, and opposed to the faithful.

"εἰς μαρτύριον πᾶσι τοις ἔθνεσι: καὶ τότε ἥξειτο τέλος. καὶ σχεδὸν ὡς ὁρῶμεν, ὁ κόσμος ἅπας τῆς περὶ χριστοῦ διδασκαλίας πεπλήρωται."

Cyril of Jerusalem thought the Preaching of the Gospel to *the whole World* so nearly complete, as to show that Christ was coming :

This gives us a measure of their strange Geographical ignorance, an ignorance often evidenced by modern Preachers and Writers. Augustine states :

" *Omnes* enim *gentes* promissae sunt, non *omnes homines omnium gentium* : non enim omnium est fides."

We cannot in these days rest satisfied with the opinion of Jerome and Augustine, that it is enough for us to preach the Gospel, and that it will be woe to those, who do not listen to it. We cannot quote the words used in the Parable of the Marriage-Feast, that "*we must compel them to come in*" with the Arm of the Flesh, murder, tortures (the advice of Augustine of Hippo), and the confiscation of property, all for Christ, as was the practice of Charlemagne, Olaf of Norway, or the Spanish Inquisition.

Jerome writes: "Signum Domini adventûs est Evangelium in totâ orbe praedicari, ut nullus sit excusabilis." Fifteen hundred years have passed away and the Lord has delayed His coming. We cannot conclude with those old Fathers, that the Prophecies, and the Great Commission, have been fulfilled. There are *no longer any ends of the round World*: we know approximately the area and the population of the Globe, and the fact, that in 1,900 years only one-third of that population has been converted, the large majority only nominally, and a large portion to false and degraded forms of the Teaching in Judaea. We cannot, therefore, comfort ourselves, and sit still waiting for a Millennium, and the Conversion of mankind by a Miracle. The wheels of God grind very slowly, but they grind very fine.

The Kelts, Teutons, Slavs, each adopted a separate system of Theology, separate names of Deities, separate forms of Worship: to the eye of the Philosopher they may have been the same or similar, but they were looked upon as totally different: the Greek and Roman terminology was essentially different, though the same in substance. There were in those days tribes differing from all the great recognized forms, but the Missionary of those days had no power of discrimination, and called them all, as now, "enemies of God, and children of Satan," because the Gospel had never been explained to them, and therefore they had never comprehended it.

Oh that the preaching in Judaea had come down to us undefiled, accompanied by the Gospel of John, and the Epistles of Paul! To the first generation of Christians there were no Scriptures: they had been taught the precious Idea orally, and had accepted Christ in His fulness on the testimony of the Apostles and eye-witnesses.

In the second or third generation Legends, the story of Miracles, Symbolism, forced fulfilment of Old Testament Prophecies, Allegories, Exaggerations, Apocalyptic Visions, Ritual, the Conception of a sanctified body called the "Church," and the Judaical revival of a "Priesthood," darkened the original simple words of the great Founder of the new Dispensation. Later on Worldliness, Luxury, Temporal Power, Intolerance, the Pagan Arts of Statuary, Painting, and Architecture, the carnal policy of ambitious Prelates, the arbitrary Edicts of Emperors, altered the whole character of the pure and simple Doctrines of the New Testament.

My task is completed. The followers of the new Dispensation of Jesus Christ did what the Hebrews in their early centuries and their later Diasporà never did, preached their good tidings to the Gentile World, not always wisely, or well, but continuously. The followers of the Hindu Sages, Zoroaster, and Confucius, never did so. Their Religious Conceptions were meant for themselves, and themselves only: the rest of the World might perish for what they cared.

Buddha led the way with a Universal Propagandism. Our Lord's command, five centuries later, in the same sense was unmistakable. Mahomet adopted the same fundamental principle of his teaching six centuries later still. Those must think poorly of the Power, Wisdom, and Love, of the great Controller of Human events, who can assume, that Buddha and Mahomet acted without His Permission, or that their schemes were allowed to take root in defiance of His Veto.

"*Factum valet,*" even if "*Fieri non debet.*"

V.

The Philosophical Aspect of the Idea of Metempsychósis.

The Idea of the Transmigration of the Eternal entity, called the Soul, or "Ψύχη," or "Anima," or Átma, or Ruh, into successive mortal substances, either Human, or Animal, or Vegetable, or Mineral, is neither new, nor unnoticed, in the History of Mankind, nor is it in itself unreasonable. I propose to treat it in detail:

1. Europe.

    A. Pythagoras and Empédocles.
    B. Homer.
    C. Plato.
    D. Virgil.
    E. Ovid.
    F. Lucan.
    G. Claudian.
    H. Irish Book of Balimote.

A. Pythagoras was born at Samos about 580 B.C., travelled in Egypt, and settled at Crotóna, in South Italy, about 540 B.C., the period of the return of the Hebrew from Babylon. He was the first, who adopted the title of Philosopher; started a School of Philosophy, and applied the word Κόσμος to the Universe, of which he knew so small a portion. Among others of the great Ideas, to which he gave birth, or perhaps only reduced from oral legends to writing, were these: (1) that the Soul, Ψύχη, was immortal, and it is obvious to the senses, that the body was only mortal; (2) that the immortal Soul passed from one body at its death into another. The idea was called by him Μετεμψύχωσις (Metempsychósis), or the Transmigration of the Soul from one place of habitation to another; perhaps the more perfect term would have been Μετενσωμάτωσις (Metensomatósis), as it was the body which was changed, not the Soul.

There is little doubt, that Pythagoras got his idea about the Soul from Egypt, which he had visited: that he derived it from India is out of all reason, as his Idea differs from the Indian Idea in important particulars, and from the Buddhist Idea *in toto*, while there is a resemblance of his Idea to the Egyptian Idea, both in essentials and details.

Empédocles lived at Agrigentum, in Sicily, 460 to 430 B.C. He was remarkable in his life as a thinker, and propounder of new doctrines at that particular Epoch, when the mind of man, both in the East and West, was waking up from its torpor. He gave birth to germs of Truth, which were developed in succeeding centuries by Plato and Aristotle : he propounded the doctrine of Transmigration of the Soul, possibly deriving it from Pythagoras. His end was as mysterious as his life, for he disappeared, and it was reported that he had leaped into the crater of Mount Etna. Horace writes thus :

> " Deus immortalis haberi
> Dum cupit Empédocles, ardentem frigidus Aetnam
> Insiluit."

Heráclitus Pónticus relates, that Pythagoras professed to have been once born as Athálides, the son of Hermes, and then to have obtained a boon from his father :

> " ζῶντα καὶ τελευτῶντα μνήμην ἔχειν τῶν συμβαινόντων."

Consequently he remembered the Trojan War, when, as Euphorbus, he was wounded by Menelaus ; and, as Pythagoras, he could still recognize the shield, which Menelaus had hung up in the temple of Apollo at Branchidae ; and, similarly, he remembered his subsequent birth as Hermotímus, and then as Pyrrhus, a fisherman of Delos. It is noteworthy, that his was a unique experience in Greek History. Horatius Flaccus alludes to this in his Odes, 1, xxviii, 9 :

> " habentque
> " Tartara Panthoiden *iterum* Orco
> " Demissum, quamvis clipeo Trojana refixo
> " Tempora testatus nihil ultra
> " Nervos atque cutem morti concesserat atrae."

The absence of all recollection of acts done in a former state of existence is explained by the Hindu Philosopher by the assertion, that at each death the Soul is divested of mind, understanding, and consciousness. Still, some men did recollect their former existences.

Plato, in the Dialogue of Meno, vol. I, p. 281, places the following words in the mouth of Socrates :

" Certain wise men and women spoke of a glorious Truth, that
" the Soul of man is immortal, and at one time has an end,
" which is called 'dying,' and at another time is born again, but is
" never destroyed. And the moral is, that a man ought to live
" always in perfect holiness. For in the ninth year Perséphoné
" sends the souls of those, from whom she has received the penalty
" of ancient crime, back again into the light of this World, and
" these are they, who become noble kings, and mighty men, and
" great in wisdom, and are called saintly heroes in after ages."

"The Soul, then, as being immortal, and having been born again many times, and having seen all things, that there are, whether in this World or in the World below, has Knowledge of them all: and it is no wonder, that she should be able to call to remembrance all that she ever knew about virtue, and about everything; for as all Nature is akin, and the Soul has learned all things, there is no difficulty in her eliciting, or as men say *learning*, all out of a single recollection, if a man be strenuous, and does not faint: for *all inquiry and all learning are but recollection* ('Ανάμνησις).''

If it be true that all knowledge is nothing else than reminiscence, it is surely necessary, that we must at some time have learned what we remember.

"ὅτι ἡμῖν ἡ μάθησις οὐκ ἄλλο τι ἢ ἀνάμνησις τυγχάνει οὖσα."

But this is impossible: our Soul existed before it came within the Human form. Cicero, in his "Tusculan Disputations," I, 24, writes, speaking of the Soul: " Habet primum memoriam, et eam infinitam rerum innumerabilium quam quidem Plato *Recordationem* esse vult superioris vitae."

Following the order of Jowett's Edition of Plato's Dialogues, I pass on to vol. I, "Phaedo," p. 443:

Cebes answered: " I agree, Socrates, in the greater part of what you say. But in what relates to the Soul men are apt to be incredulous: they fear that, when she has left the body, her place may be nowhere, and that on the very day of death (of the body) she may be destroyed and perish. If she could only hold together, and be herself, when she is released from the evils of the body, there would be good reason to hope, Socrates, that what you say is true. But much persuasion and many arguments are required in order to prove that, when the man is dead, the Soul still exists, and has any force or intelligence."

Socrates replied: " Whether the Souls of men after death are, or are not, in the World below, is a question which may be argued in this way. The ancient Doctrine affirms, that they go hence into the other World, and return hither, and are born from the dead. So our Souls must exist in the other World, for, if not, how could they have been born again ? But as there is no evidence of this, other arguments will have to be adduced."

Socrates then works out a long argument to prove, that not every thing living is born of the dead, and the Soul will exist after death as well as before birth: then comes the greater question to decide what becomes of the Soul which leaves the body *pure*, and the Soul which leaves the body *impure*. This brings out the terrible theory of Retribution, and at p. 459, Socrates tells us that the Souls of men who followed after gluttony, and wantonness, and drunkenness, will pass into Asses, and animals of that sort, and the Souls of those, who have chosen the portion of injustice and tyranny, will pass into wolves or hawks; and the Souls of those, who have practised the civil and social virtues, which are called Temperance and Justice, will pass into some gentle social nature like their own, such as that of bees, wasps, and ants, or even back again into the form of man, and just and moderate men will spring from them; and he, who is a philosopher or lover of learning, and abstains from all fleshly lusts, and refuses to give himself up to them, is alone permitted to obtain the Divine Nature.

Socrates opens out, p. 457, another solemn delusion, which has preyed on the Human mind for centuries, and still maintains its grasp:

"The Soul, which has been polluted and is impure at the
" time of her departure, and is the companion and servant of the
" body always, and is fascinated with the desires and pleasures of
" the body . . . . such a Soul is held fast by the corporeal
" element, and is depressed and dragged back again into the
" visible World, because she is afraid of the invisible World and
" the World below: prowling about tombs and sepulchres, in
" the neighbourhood of which are seen ghostly apparitions of Souls,
" which have not departed pure, but are cloyed with sight and
" therefore visible, and they continue to wander, until through the
" craving of the corporeal, which never leaves them, they are im-
" prisoned finally in another body. And they may be supposed to
" find their prisons in the same natures, which they had in their
" former lives."

Milton, in his "Comus," re-echoes this idea (l. 463):

" But when Lust,
" By unchaste looks, loose gestures, and foul talk,
" But most by lewd and lavish act of sin,
" Lets in defilement to the inward parts,
" The Soul grows clotted by contagion,
" Imbodies, and imbrutes, till she quite lose
" The divine property of her first being.
" Such are those thick and gloomy shadows damp,
" Oft seen in charnel-vaults and sepulchres,
" Lingering, and sitting by a new-made grave,
" As loth to leave the body that it loved,
" And link'd itself, by carnal sensuality,
" To a degenerate, and degraded state."

Plato, in his "Phaedrus," returns to the subject (vol. ii, pp. 125, 126). I quote Jowett's "Introduction," page 80, as condensing the subject. Socrates is the speaker: "The Soul is Immortal, for she
" is the source of all motion, both in herself and others. Her form

"may be described in a figure as a composite nature made up of a charioteer, and a pair of winged steeds. The steeds of the gods are immortal, but the steeds of the Soul are, one mortal, and the other Immortal. The Immortal Soul soars up into the Heavens, but the mortal drops her plumes and settles upon the earth.

"On a certain day Zeus goes forth in a winged chariot, and an array of gods and demigods, and of Human Souls, follows him; the mortal steed of the Soul sinks down to the earth. Yet, if the Soul has followed in the train of her god, and once beheld Truth, she is preserved harmless; but if she drops her wing and falls to the earth, then she takes the form of a man. The Soul, which has seen most of the Truth, passes into a Philosopher, or a Lover; that which has seen Truth in a second degree, into a King, or Warrior, and so on to the ninth degree. In all these conditions the lot of him, who lives righteously is improved, and the lot of him who lives unrighteously deteriorates. At the end of every thousand years the Soul has another choice, and may go upwards or downwards, may descend into a beast, or return again to the form of man. But the form of man can only be acquired at all by those, who have once beheld the Truth, for the Soul of man alone apprehends the Universal, and this is the recollection, ἀνάμνησις, of that Knowledge, which she obtained when in the company of the god. Ten thousand years must elapse before the Souls of men in general can regain their first lot, and have their wings restored to them. But the Soul of a Philosopher, or a Lover, who has three times in succession chosen the better life, may receive wings, and go her way in three thousand years."

In the "Timaeus," vol. iii, p. 624, we read: "The great Creator considered, that a perfect World could not exist without mortals. If they were created by Him, and received Life from Him, they would be on equality with the gods: the inferior gods were therefore ordered to form animals, and the Creator would supply the divine and immortal part. Accordingly, Souls were created as numerous as the stars, and each Soul had a star, but was implanted in a body: they had certain passions, but, if they conquered, then they would live righteously; and, if they were conquered by them, unrighteously. He, who lived well during his appointed time, was to return to his star, and there he would have a suitable existence; but if he failed in attaining this, in the second generation he would pass into a woman, and, should he not desist from his evil ways, he would be changed into some brute beast, who resembled him in his evil ways, and would not cease from his lusts, and transformation, until he returned to the form of his first and better nature."

Again, at page 675 we read: "Thus were created women, but the race of birds was created out of innocent, light-minded men, who, although their minds were directed towards Heaven, "imagined in their simplicity, that the clearest demonstration of the things above would be obtained by sight: these were transformed into birds and grew feathers instead of hair. The reason why quadrupeds and polypods were created is, that the Creator gave the more senseless of them the more support, that they might be attracted to the earth. The inhabitants of the water were made out of the most entirely ignorant and senseless beings." This and much more is narrated, and Plato closes the Dialogue with the following words: "These are the laws, by which animals pass into one another, both now and ever changing, as they lose or gain wisdom and folly."

Strabo, Book IV, writes:

" Ἀφθάρτους τὰς ψυχὰς λέγουσι."

Valerius Maximus, Book V, and Diodorus, Book VI, could also be quoted.

In the Introduction to the "History of Religion" (1896), is a chapter (xxii) on the "Transmigration of Souls," by Dr. F. B. Jevons, of Durham, no mean authority on such subjects, and being lately published, it may be presumed, that it is an up-to-date view of the subject. The twelve pages of this Chapter go over ground not necessarily part of the argument, but a knowledge of which is necessary to arrive at an understanding of the germs, from which the Idea rose.

1. The general Idea of Barbarians was, that after death the individual "*Homo*" rejoined his "totem," and assumed the shape of the plant or animal, which was worshipped as the "totem."

II. As the Religious Idea of the Human race developed, more advanced Ideas came into existence, one of which was the Idea of "Retribution in a future state," for acts done during life. These two Ideas in some communities existed side by side, notably in Egypt and India: this state of things may have lasted for a long period, but the two Ideas acted and reacted on each other, and at last the artificial combination of the "Retribution" theory with Totemism produced in Egypt a real theory of Metempsychósis, but an incomplete one: (1) it was only the wicked, who were doomed to Transmigration; (2) the Soul of a man migrated into animals, returning finally to Human form; (3) there was no escape from this cycle, but, when the Human form was again attained, the Soul had another trial and another chance of becoming Osiris, which was the Egyptian formula for Eternal Happiness.

In India the process was different: the Idea of Transmigration was extended to the virtuous, as well as the wicked, who passed into animals or men according to their deeds and knowledge. Here is the *genuine* theory of Metempsychósis, or Transmigration of Souls; and man has been introduced into the list of Metamorphoses.

All men were born again: the good had a good birth, and the bad a bad one, according to their deeds and deserts: there was no escape from this environment; whether the Soul behaved badly or well he had to be reborn.

Thus far the Brahman: the Buddhist went further; with him there was no god, no Immortal Soul, and there could be no Transmigration of Souls, but a transmission of Karma or Character (not Soul): the extinction of cravings for delights of the body, or Nirvána, was the object of the Buddhist: this will be described further on.

The accomplished authoress of an Article in the *Edinburgh Review*, April, 1897, "Sculptured Tombs of Hellas," makes the following important suggestions :

" At Athens and Delphi the doctrines of Orphism took strong
" hold; but it was in Lower Italy, owing to the teaching of
" Pythagoras, and Empédocles, that they developed most completely,
" and issued in a Totemistic Doctrine of the Transmigration of
" Souls. Many a barbarian believed, that after Death he would
" pass into the shape of the sacred animal, who had been his token
" (Totem) in this world.

" The Inscription on one Greek vase from Apulia, and on golden
" tablets from Thurii and Peletia in Italy, suggest something more :
" ' Thou wilt feel a stream of cold water flowing from the mere
" ' of Mnemósyné: in front of it stand guards. Say: "I am the child
" ' of Earth, and starry sky:

" ' Γῆς παῖς εἰμι καὶ οὐρανοῦ ἀστερόεντος.

" ' I am of heavenly birth ; I am parched and faint with thirst; give
" ' me cool water from the mere of Mnemósyné," and they will give
" ' thee the divine water to drink.' "

The Doctrine is clear: the initiated Soul may not drink of the oblivious waters of Lethé : it is reborn by remembering again, by virtue of the Divine Life in him: this is the Doctrine of Plato's Ἀνάμνησις. Immortality is but the reassertion of the Divine Life in Man.

In their groping after the Future, Men stretched out their hands into the dark abyss, and as they advanced in intellect, their speculations were more daring. We must speak and write humbly, for in this Nineteenth century A.D., we have no knowledge, only that Faith, the "evidence of things not seen" (Hebrews, xi, 1). The two Theories were :

(1) The continuance of this life in another World.
(2) Retribution.

In the first theory the Future Life was very much as the old one: the Chief required his wives, his servants, his jewels, his armour, and his food; ancient Tombs reveal this. In the second theory the Future Life depended on conduct in the present. Later ages struck out new Ideas:

(1) Absorption of the Soul, and practical destruction of its individuality.
(2) The Transmigration of the Soul into a new body.
(3) The wandering of the Soul, free from its corporeal covering, in its old earthly environment.

Let us dispose of the last alternative first: it lies outside the limits of an Essay on the Transmigration of Souls from one Earthly tenement to another, such as was the case of these poor Souls, as described by Socrates in the "Phaedo," and Milton in the "Comus," quoted above at p. 956.

The following quotation from Shakespeare's "Measure for Measure," III, Scene 1:

". . . . and the delighted Spirit
"To bathe in fiery floods, or to reside
"In thrilling region of thick-ribbed ice;
"To be imprison'd in the viewless winds,
"And blown with restless violence round about
"The pendent world: 't is too horrible!"

In uncultured tribes the Idea was, that the Soul would not remain quiet unless proper funeral rites were performed to the poor body: this is brought out strongly in the Sixth Book of Virgil's "Aeneid," 337: the boatman Charon would not ferry across the Styx those, who had not been properly buried. Moreover, in some cases the Spirit came back, and vented its wrath upon its nearest relations. This is the real motive of the worship of Ancestors in China.

The Greek and Roman Poets, Homer and Virgil, reflecting the beliefs of their age, give us a most unphilosophical and unsatisfactory substitute for either of the three alternatives.

The Elysian Fields are certainly a somewhat higher type than the sensual Paradise of Mahomet, or the Purgatory of the Church of Rome. Some very bad cases lived in perpetual torture, though the story of Tantalus and Sisyphus both seem allegories of the result of particular vices; but the position of those, who were deemed good, seems the most unhappy. Dido still had her sorrows, from which she sought consolation from her dead husband, to whose memory she had been unfaithful. Achilles mourned the change from activity to hopeless idleness, but he retained memory of the past:

> "Quam vellent aethere in alto
> Nunc et pauperiem et duros perferre labores!"
>
> VIRGIL: *Aeneid*, vi, 436.

> "Μὴ δή μοι θάνατόν γε παραύδα, φαίδιμ' Ὀδυσσεῦ.
> "Βουλοίμην κ' ἐπάρουρος ἐὼν θητευέμεν ἄλλῳ,
> "Ἢ πᾶσιν νεκύεσσι καταφθιμένοισιν ἀνάσσειν."
>
> HOMER: *Odyssey*, xi, 488.

> "Scoff not at death," he answered, "noble Chief.
> "Rather would I in the Sun's warmth divine
> "Serve a poor churl, who drags his days in grief,
> "Than the whole lordship of the dead were mine."
>
> WORSLEY's Translation.

When such were the conceptions in the time of Homer with regard to the future condition of the dead, even those who were conventionally deemed "good," there could have been no contemporary Idea of Transmigration of Souls. Centuries later, when Virgil handled the subject, the Idea as described above had crept in; the World had advanced, and Pythagoras and Plato had spoken, opening out new vistas of thought.

Virgil, in the Sixth Book of the "Aeneid," writes (1. 735):

> "Quin et, supremo cum lumine vita reliquit,
> "Non tamen omne malum miseris, nec funditus omnes
> "Corporeae excedunt pestes: penitusque necesse est
> "Multa diu concreta modis inolescere miris.
> "*Ergo exercentur poenis*, veterumque malorum
> "Supplicia expendunt. Aliae panduntur inanes,
> "Suspensae, ad ventos: aliis sub gurgite vasto
> "Infectum eluitur scelus, aut exuritur igni.
> "Quisque suos patimur Manes: exinde per amplum
> "Mittimur Elysium, et pauci laeta arva tenemus.
> "Donec longa dies, perfecto temporis orbe,
> "Concretam exemit labem, purumque reliquit
> "Aethereum sensum, atque, auraï simplicis ignem.
> "Has omnes, ubi mille rotam volvere per annos,
> "Lethaeum ad fluvium Deus evocat agmine magno;
> "Scilicet *immemores* supera ut convexa revisant,
> "Rursus et incipiant in corpora velle reverti."

Anchises showed to Aeneas some of his descendants, who, having been freed from the stain of former lives, and having drunk of the waters of Lethé, were about to assume new forms, and enter the battle of life again: this called forth Aeneas' sad remark:

"O pater, anne aliquas ad coelum hinc ire putandum est
"Sublimes animas, iterumque in tarda reverti
"Corpora? Quae lucis miseris tam dira cupido?"

But Virgil, in the "Aeneid," III, 20-40, describes the Transmigration of a comparatively innocent man, Polydorus, son of King Priam of Troy, into a tree overhanging his tomb, from the branches of which blood flowed, when they were cut with a knife, and the unfortunate Soul thus imprisoned had the power of recognizing those, who amputated his limbs, and speaking with an intelligible voice:

"Gemitus lacrimabilis imo
"Auditur tumulo, et vox reddita fertur ad aures:
"Quid miserum, Aenea, laceras? jam parce sepulto;
"Parce pias scelerare manus. Non me tibi Troja
"Externum tulit: aut cruor hic de stipite manat.
"Heu! fuge crudeles terras, fuge littus avarum.
"Nam Polydorus ego: hic confixum ferrea texit
"Telorum seges, et jaculis increvit acutis."

Ovid, in his "Metamorphoses," about the date of the Christian era, naturally touches on this subject:

"O genus attonitum gelidâ formidine mortis!
"Quid Styga, quid tenebras, quid numine vana, timetis,
"Materiem vatum, falsique piacula mundi?
"Corpora sive rogus flammâ, seu tabe vetustas
"Abstulerit, mala posse pati non ulla putetis.
"Morte carent animae: semperque priore relictâ
"Sede, novis domibus habitant, vivuntque, receptae.
"Ipse ego, nam memini, Trojani tempore belli,
"Panthoides Euphorbus eram, cui pectore quondam
"Sedit in adverso gravis hasta minoris Atridae,
"Cognovi clypeum, laevae gestaminae nostrae,
"Nuper Abanteis templo Junonis in Argis.
"Omnia mutantur: nihil interit. Errat, et illinc
"Huc venit: hinc illuc, et quoslibet occupat artûs
"Spiritus, èque feris humana in corpora transit,
"Inque feras noster, nec tempore deperit ullo,
"Utque novis facilis signatur cera figuris,
"Nec manet, ut fuerat, nec formas servat easdem,
"Sed *tamen ipsa eadem est: animam sic semper eandem*
"*Esse*."

(xv, 153-172.)

Lucan, in his "Pharsalia," I, 454, A.D. 60, writes thus with regard to the Druids:

> " Vobis auctoribus umbrae
> " Non tacitas Erebi sedes, Ditisque profundi
> " Pallida regna petunt: regit idem spiritus artûs
> " Orbe alio: longae, canitis si cognita, vitae
> " Mors media est. Certe populi quos despicit Arctos
> " Felices errore suo, quos ille, timorum
> " Maximus, haud urget leti metus. Inde ruendi
> " In ferrum mens prona viris, animaeque capaces
> " Mortis, et ignarum rediturae parcere vitae."

Julius Caesar, in his "De Bello Gallico," Book VI, Section xiii, writes about the ancient Druids of Britain:

" In primis haec volunt persuadere, non *interire animas*, sed *ab aliis post mortem transire* ad alios : atque hoc maximé ad virtutem excitari putant, metu mortis neglecto."

It is clear, that it was impressed on the thoughtful Philosopher, that some explanation must be found of the caprices of Human fortune, for the holy and good are subjected to unmerited suffering, while good gifts are showered upon most unworthy recipients. Claudian, A.D. 400, remarked this phenomenon, and marvelled:

> " Saepe mihi dubiam tenuit sententia mentem,
> " Curarent Superi terras, an nullus inesset
> " Rector, et incerto fluerent mortalia casu :
> " Nam, cum dispositi quaesissem foedera mundi,
> " Praescriptosque maris fines, amnisque meatus,
> " Et lucis, noctisque, vices: tunc omnia rebar
> " Concilio firmata Dei :
> " Sed cum res Hominum tantâ caligine volvi
> " Aspiciam, laetosque diu florere nocentes,
> " Vexarique pios, rursus labefacta cadebat
> " Religio."

And the same uncertainty prevails to the present hour.

There is a curious Irish Legend recorded in the "Book of Balimote," 1400 A.D., which certainly reads as if the notion of Transmigration was held at some previous period:

> " Tuan, son of Cairill, as we are told,
> " Was freed from sin by Jesus :
> " One hundred years complete he lived,
> " He lived in blooming manhood.
>
> " Three hundred years in the shape of a wild ox
> " He lived on the open extensive plains :
> " Two hundred and fifty years he lived
> " In the shape of a wild boar.

"Three hundred years he was still in the flesh
"In the shape of an old bird:
"One hundred delightful years he lived
"In the shape of a salmon in the flood.

"A fisherman caught him in his net,
"He brought it to the king's palace:
"When the bright salmon was there seen,
"The Queen immediately longed for it.

"It was forthwith dressed for her,
"Which she alone ate entire:
"The beauteous Queen became pregnant,
"The issue of which was Tuan."

---

2. Non-European Countries.

A. Egypt.
B. North American Redmen.
C. The Hebrew.
D. The Manichean.
E. The Mahometan.
F. The Hindu.
G. The Buddhist.

A. *Egypt.*

Herodotus, B.C. 470, and therefore anterior to Plato, writes (II, 123): "The Egyptians were the first to broach the opinion, "that the Soul of man is Immortal, and that, when the body dies, "it enters in the form of the animal, which is born at the moment, "thence passing from one animal into another, until it has circled "through the forms of all the creatures, which tenant the earth, "water, and air, after which it enters again into a human frame, "and is born anew. The whole period of Transmigration is three "thousand years. There are Greek writers, some of an earlier "date, some of a later, who have borrowed this doctrine from the "Egyptians, and put it forward as their own."

It is unnecessary to state here any further details with regard to the Egyptian Idea; it is sufficient to refer to the standard authorities on the subject of Egyptian Antiquities.

B. North American Redmen.

With a view of showing the universality of the Idea, I merely refer to the "Golden Bough" of Mr. Frazer (i, 39, 61 ; ii, 97), in which mention is made of the Idea of Souls of dead animals occupying trees, and the Soul of a man in a turtle. The Red Indians believed, that the Soul animating the body of an infant was the Soul of some deceased person.

From Tylor's "Primitive Man" we gather, that enslaved Negroes have been known to commit suicide, in order that they may revive in their native land.

The aborigines of Australia hold white men to be the ghosts of their own dead, in the simple formula: "Black fellow tumble down, jump up white fellow."

With regard to this last view, it may be well to quote Henry Stanley's account of his meeting with four white men, who had come out from Embomma, on the West Coast of Africa, to welcome him at the close of his journey through the Dark Continent : " The " sight of the pale faces of the Merchants gave me the slightest " suspicion of an involuntary shiver. The pale colour, after so " long gazing on the rich black, and richer bronze, had something " of an unaccountable ghastliness. In fact, they looked like the " ghosts of dead Africans." (Vol. ii, p. 462.)

C. *The Hebrew.*

The Idea of the Hebrew on the subject of Eschatology was exceedingly elementary previous to the return from exile. Their World was a three-storied house : they dwelt on the first floor ; above them in the clouds was the second story, the Heavens, to which only two men had ever reached, Enoch and Elijah ; in the ground-story was the Sheol, or Hades, in which all dwelt promiscuously, for Samuel, when he was summoned up to the first floor, told Saul, that on the morrow he would be down with him in Sheol : good and bad, without difference.

There is little doubt that some of the Hebrew Sects held the Idea of Transmigration of Souls. We come across the Idea in the Christian Scriptures of a possible existence of a former life. We know, that a Future State was not a Hebrew dogma at the time of our Lord, as the Sadducees openly denied it. Now when the Sadducees, tempting the Lord on the subject of the Resurrection, asked Him whose wife would the woman be of the seven brothers, our Lord rebuked them : " Ye do err, not knowing the Scriptures " ; and yet it does not appear an unreasonable question from their point of view, and many a Christian tombstone records the wish of a bereaved husband, possibly a husband of two wives, to be united to the lost companions of his life.

But when the Pharisees. pointing to a man who was born blind, asked him: "Master, who did sin, this man or his Parents, that he was born blind?" our Lord did not rebuke them, nor did He point out, that the question was a foolish one, as no man could possibly sin before his birth, but He replied: "Neither *has this man sinned*, nor his parents, but that the works of God might be made manifest in him."

Bishop Lightfoot of Durham notices the speculations of the Rabbis on this subject in his Commentary: one was, that sin was possible already in the womb, since the embryo in its later stages was possessed of consciousness. This seems hard on the newborn babe, who, by the theory of Augustine of Hippo, is already saddled with the "*peccatum originale*" of his reputed ancestor Adam.

It is anyhow clear, that this question on the part of the Pharisees implies the Idea of Metempsychósis, or they would never have propounded such a problem, and our Lord, in His Wisdom, did not satisfy their curiosity. The question is left an open one.

I am informed by a very competent authority, a Medical man, who lived among the Hebrews many years in Palestine, that the common Idea of the modern Hebrew is, that at the moment of a child's birth, an Angel strikes it on the mouth, causing it to forget all that it knew in a previous existence, and the dimple on the upper lip is the result of the blow." I add a quotation from Shechter, "Studies in Judaism," 1896, pp. 345–347:

"These legends with reference to the embryo period in the life
" of a child, are chiefly based on the notion of the pre-existence of
" the Soul. . . . . Care is taken to make the child forget all
" it has seen and heard in these upper regions in its state of pre-
" existence. Before it enters the World an angel strikes it on the
" upper lip, and all its knowledge and wisdom disappear at once.
" The pit in the upper lip is a result of this stroke, which is also
" the cause why children cry, when they are born."

Clearly children do inherit some of the results of the sins of their parents in diseased bodies: it may be possible, that they inherit the results of their own sins in a former existence. Those eyes, which once glanced lustfully, cruelly, or enviously, are now closed to the outer world. This is a mere hypothesis, but it is right to consider it. There is nothing inconsistent with, nor opposed to, Revealed Religion in the Idea, that to an individual Soul the opportunity should be given of repeated incarnations. Gradually, in this way, defects of character of individual Souls would be subdued, and they would be more fit for the Kingdom of Heaven. Had the very root-conception of the matter been wrong, and fundamentally wicked, our Lord would have condemned it. Notoriously by Mosaic Law the sins of the Parents were deemed to be visited on the children: one portion of the argument of the Pharisees was sound, though contrary to elementary modern ideas of Justice, and condemned by

Ezekiel (cap. xviii) at the time of the Captivity: if the other portion had been wickedly wrong, or ridiculous, our Lord would scarcely have failed to condemn it, as He never spared those, who tempted Him by improper questions.

If there had not existed among the Hebrews of that time an Idea of the possibility of a Soul returning to a new body after an interval of more or less length, how is it that our Lord was identified as Elijah or one of the Prophets, since whose death centuries had passed? and, still more markedly, what could have induced Herod to suppose, that Jesus was identical with John the Baptist, whom he a short time before had himself beheaded?

In truth, Nature exhibits unlimited examples of decay in the works of Creation, and regeneration: there may be a channel of compensation for unmerited (as far as Human eye can see) suffering, and a vengeance taken upon neglected opportunities, abused privileges, and intolerable tyranny of lustful Power.

It may be part of the Divine discipline (as it was, that the Soul of Dives in torments should look across an abyss, and see the Soul of Lazarus in bliss) to suffer such sinning Souls to assume in a second birth the very reverse of their previous lot, with the possibility of atoning for their gross sins.

The Apocalyptic writings betray the yearning of the heart of man to know something of the Future. The Revelation of John has not helped us much to pierce the veil: at any rate, in the Nineteenth century after Christ we know with certainty as little as was known in the First, but the World has lasted long enough to prove, that Paul's anticipations of the early coming of Christ were vague and unsupported by fact. Millions have passed away to their unknown home, but the Lord has delayed His coming, notwithstanding that Wickedness does abound.

I approach with reverent reserve the Miracle of our Lord, by which an evil spirit passed out of a man, and at its own petition entered the bodies of a herd of swine; that is to say, it subdivided itself by the occupation of many bodies of the herd, while, although consisting of many individualities, as a Roman Legion, it had dwelt in one Human frame. This is one of the difficult portions of the New Testament. It does not necessarily follow, that the population of Gádara were Hebrew: the presumption based on Geography, and the fact that they kept herds of swine, which were unclean to the Hebrew, is, that they were not. In their Pagan minds they had conceived the Idea, that malignant demons could take possession of the bodies of living men, and impel them to frantic movements. At any rate, this story also is based on the existence of an Idea at that time prevalent in Syria, that Souls and Spirits could migrate from one mortal tenement to another. The very notion of such a thing in modern times would be rejected without argument: not the Miracle, but the Human circumstances, which preceded and followed the Miracle.

The references in the late work called "Zohar" to the Idea of Metempsychósis, are collected by Gratz ("History of the Jews," vol. iv). We get some clue to the thoughts of the Hebrews on this subject from the following quotations from Josephus, whose date, and means of information, are so well known:

I. ("Antiquities of the Jews," Book XVIII, cap. i, § 3.) "The Pharisees believe, that Souls have an immortal vigour in them, and that under the earth there will be rewards and punishments according as they have lived virtuously or viciously in this life; and the latter are to be detained in an everlasting prison, but that the former shall have *power to revive and live again*: on account of which doctrines they are able greatly to persuade the body of the people."

II. ("Wars of the Jews," Book II, cap. viii, § 14.) "The Pharisees say, that all Souls are incorruptible, but that the *Souls of good men only are removed into other bodies*, but that the Souls of bad men are subject to eternal punishment. The Sadducees take away the belief of the Immortal duration of the Soul, and the punishments and rewards in Hades."

III. ("Wars of the Jews," Book III, cap. viii, § 5.) "Do not you know, that those, who depart out of this life according to the Law of Nature, and pay that debt, which was received from God, when He that lent it is pleased to require it back again, enjoy eternal fame: that their homes, and their posterity, are sure, that their Souls are pure and obedient, and obtain a most holy place in Heaven, whence in the revolution of ages they *are again sent into pure bodies*; while the Souls of those, who have acted madly against themselves, are received by the darkest place in Hades."

In an article by Dr. Ginsburg, in Smith's "Dictionary of Christian Biography," vol. I, p. 361, word "Kabbalah," we read as follows:

"It is an absolute condition of the Soul to return to the Infinite Source, from which it emanated, after developing on earth the perfections, the germs whereof are implanted in it. If the Soul, after assuming a Human body, and its *first* sojourn on earth, fails to acquire that experience, for which it descends from Heaven, and becomes contaminated by sin, it *must reinhabit a body again, and again*, until it is able to ascend in a purified state. This transmigration, however, is restricted to three times. If two Souls on their residence in Human bodies are still too weak to acquire the necessary experience, they are united, and *sent into one body*, in order that by their combined efforts they may be able to learn that, which they were too feeble to effect separately."

Paul, in the Romans, ix, 11, writes: "For the children *being not yet born, neither having done any good or evil*," to justify the Doctrine of Election.

D. *The Manichean.*

The Manicheans held the Doctrine in various forms, as detailed in "Acta Martyrum," 1748 A.D. (Syriac and Latin): it is stated at page 203, that they supposed that the Souls of men entered ants. Neander, in his Church History, II, 218, alluded to it.

E. *The Mahometan.*

We should scarcely have expected to find traces of the Idea in a Religion so modern, so universal, and free from the old-world Ideas, as the Mahometan; yet they are found. Arabian writers allude to three forms of Transmigration. The shifting of Souls into green birds was recognized (Baidawi, Commentary on "Súra," III, 165) as coming near to this Idea.

A scholarly friend has helped me to the following quatrain from Omar Khaiyyam:

آن بـسادہ کـه قــابل صورھات بذات

گاھــی حیــون میشود وگاھــی نبـات

تا ظـن نبری کــه نیست گـردد ھیات

موصوف بذاتست اگر نیست صفات

" That essence, which is inherently fit for form,
" Sometimes is an animal, and sometimes a plant:
" Think not, that form becomes non-existent;
" It is known as existing, although there may not be any shape."

I am indebted to my friend, Professor Edward G. Browne, of Pembroke College, Cambridge, so well known for his Mahometan studies, for the following important communication:

" The question as to the prevalence of the doctrine of Trans-
" migration of Souls in Mahometan countries is a difficult but
" very interesting one. Although the belief appears to be held,
" and to have been held, by many sects in Islám, especially
" the ultra-Shi'ite sects of Persia, it is a fact, that they mostly
" repudiate it formally, i.e., they will not admit that they hold the
" *tanásukh-i-arwáh* (تناسخ ارواح), which is the technical term in
" Arabic for this doctrine. But they believe in what they call
" the ' *Rij'at* ' (رجعت) or 'Return,' which is to us almost
" undistinguishable. The Bábí, for instance, speak of the 're-
" turn' in this 'Manifestation' or dispensation of the saints and

"sinners of former dispensations. I saw at Kirmán, in Persia, a Bábí woman, who believed herself to be a 'return' of Kurratu'l-'Ayn, the martyr-poetess. And I have cited in my Translation of the *New History* of the Báb (Cambridge, 1893, pp. 334–338 and 357) instances of this belief, especially one (p. 338), where a *dog* is declared by a Bábí saint to be the 'return' of a certain unbeliever. These heterodox sects generally fight shy of admitting, that they hold the doctrine of *Metempsychósis* under its ordinary name, *tanásukh*, but, under the name of *rij'at*, hold a doctrine, which it seems impossible to distinguish therefrom. In the next number of the *Journal of the Royal Asiatic Society* I hope that a paper will appear, which I have written on a little-known sect called the *Hurúfí*, which flourished in the Fifteenth and Sixteenth centuries of our era in Persia and Turkey, in which paper I discuss this matter more or less. In Mahometan philosophical works, even modern ones, such as the *Asrár-i-Hikam* of Háji Mullá Hádi of Sabzawár, a chapter is generally consecrated to the formal refutation of the doctrine, which is therefore recognized as existing in Mahometan countries.

"My impression is, that nearly all the extreme Shi'ite sects, which had their origin in Persia, really hold the doctrine. There are some well-known lines in the *Másnavi*, which look like an enunciation of the doctrine, though orthodox Mahometans try to explain them away. They run:

"'I died from the Mineral, and became a Plant: I died from the Plant, and reappeared as an Animal.

"'I died from the animal state, and became a man: why, then, should I fear? when did I ever grow less by dying?

"'Next time I shall die from humanity, that I may clothe myself in wings with the Angels.

"'Beyond the Angels, too, must I rise: *all things shall perish save His Face!*'

"This is the general sense of the lines, and there is a very similar passage in Ibn Yamín. I have discussed the way, in which they interpret the doctrine in my 'Year amongst the Persians.'"

F. Hindu.

The Hindu Sages, with their speculative Genius, will find a cause for everything, or at least invent one. How came the necessity of Transmigration into existence? They had the undoubted fact, that men did die, and the strong conviction, that the Soul did not die. I quote the following from the Satapátha-Bráhmana:

" The gods live constantly in fear of Death,
" The mighty Ender, so with tedious rites
" They worshipped, and repeated Sacrifice,
" Till they became Immortal. Then the Ender
" Said to the gods : ' As ye have made yourselves
" Imperishable, so will men endeavour
" To free themselves from me : what portion, then,
" Shall I possess in man ?' The gods replied :
" ' Henceforth no being shall become Immortal
" In his own body : this his mortal frame
" Shalt thou still seize : this shall remain thine own,
" This shall become perpetually thy food ;
" And even if he through religious acts
" Henceforth attains to Immortality,
" Shall first present his body, Death, to thee.' "

(" Indian Wisdom," p. 34.)

Transmigration became the terrible nightmare of Indian Metaphysicians: all their efforts were directed to getting rid of this oppressive scare. As the embodied Soul, says the Bhágavad Gíta, moves swiftly on through boyhood, youth, and age, so will it pass through other forms hereafter. The one engrossing problem is : How is a man to break this iron chain of repeated existences ? how is he to shake off all personality ? how is he to return to complete absorption (*sayujya*) into pure unconscious Spirit ? or, failing this, is he to work his way through successive births to any of the three inferior conditions of bliss ?

(1) Living in the same sphere with the personal God (Sálokya).
(2) Close proximity to that God (Sámípya).
(3) Assimilation to the likeness of that God (Sárupya).

Professor Rhys Davids, in his "Hibbert Lectures," p. 80, expresses his opinion, that the Arians, when they entered India from the North-West, did not bring the idea of Metempsychósis with them. It is not mentioned in the Veda. In one of the earlier Upanishads, 600 B.C., we read : " Those, whose conduct has been good, will quickly attain some good birth, birth as a Bráhmana, or a Kshatriya, or a Vaisya."

In the Kaushítaki Bráhmana Upanishad we read: "All, who
" depart from this world, go to the Moon : in the dark fort-
" night the Moon sends them forth into new births: they are born
" either as a worm, or a grasshopper, or a fish, or a bird, or a lion,
" or a boar, or a serpent, or a tiger, or a man, or some animal,
" according to their deeds and their knowledge."

It is possible that the Arian immigrants, long after their entry into India, derived the idea from the Non-Arian occupants of the Gangetic Valley, whom they found in possession on their arrival.

The Hindu, being essentially of a more dreamy temperament, gives evidence of this Idea of the Soul having recollection of something, that has happened in a previous state of existence. That a man should in his new Birth recollect the circumstances of his previous incarnation, is a common feature in Legends, but Manu (IV, 148) specially notices this capacity as the reward of a self-denying and pious life. I quote a poetical translation from a passage in the Vishnu Puránu, which I made at Banda, in North India, as far back as 1853:

THE HINDU NOTION OF A FUTURE STATE.

[*From the Sanskrit.*]

MAITRÉYA (the Pupil).

" Parásura, you've told me
" All that I wished to hear,
" How out of chaos sprang this
" God-made hemisphere.

" How zone on zone, and sphere on sphere,
" In ever-varying forms,
" The wondrous egg of Brahma
" With living creatures swarms.

" All great and small, all small and great,
" On their own acts depend:
" All their terrestrial vanities
" In punishment must end.

" Released from Yáma, they are born
" As men, as beasts, again ;
" And thus in countless circles still
" Revolving still remain.

" Tell me, oh! tell me what I ask,
" What you alone can tell :
" By what acts only mortal men
" Can free themselves from Hell ?"

PARÁSURA (the Teacher).

" Listen, Maitréya, best of men :
    " The question you have brought
" Was once by royal Nákula
    " Of aged Bhisma sought.

" And thus the hoary sage replied :
    " Listen, my Prince, this tale
" A Brahman guest once told me
    " From far Kalinga's vale.

" He from an ancient Múni too
    " The wondrous secret gained,
" In whose clear mind of former births
    " The memory remained.

" Never before had human ear
    " The tale mysterious heard :
" Such as it was I tell it you,
    " Repeating word for word.

" As from the coil of mortal birth
    " Released the Múni lay,
" He heard the awful King of Death
    " Thus to his menials say :

" Touch not, I charge thee, anyone,
    " Whom Vishnú has let loose :
" On Madhu-súdan's followers
    " Cast not the fatal noose.

" Brahma appointed me to rule
    " Poor erring mortals' fate,
" Of evil and uncertain good
    " The balance regulate.

" But he, who chooses Vishnú
    " As spiritual guide,
" Slave of a mightier lord than me,
    " Can spurn me in my pride.

" As gold is of one substance still,
    " Assume what form it can,
" So Vishnú is the selfsame power
    " As Beast, as God, or Man.

" And as the drops of watery spray,
" Raised by the wind on high,
" Sink slowly down again to earth
" When calm pervades the sky,

" So particles of source divine
" Created forms contain :
" When that disturbance is composed,
" They reunite again.

" But tell us, Master, they replied,
" How shall thy slaves descry
" Those who with heart and soul upon
" The mighty Lord rely ?

" Oh! they are those, who truly love
" Their neighbours, them you'll know,
" Who never from their duty swerve,
" And would not hurt their foe.

" Whose hearts are undefiled
" By soil of Kali's age,
" Who let not others' hoarded wealth
" Their envious thoughts engage.

" No more can Vishnú there abide,
" Where evil passions sway,
" Than glowing heat of fire reside
" In the moon's cooling ray.

" But those, who covet others' wealth,
" Whose hearts are hard in sin,
" And those, whose low degraded souls
" Pride rampant reigns within ;

" Whoever with the wicked sit,
" And daily frauds prepare,
" Who duties to their friends forget :
" Vishnú has nothing there.

" Such were the orders, that the King
" Of Hell his servants gave :
" For Vishnú his true followers
" From death itself can save."

I now quote from the well-known play of "Sakóntala," by Kalidása. I give the English translation, and then the original: "When a being, in other respects happy, becomes conscious of an ardent longing on seeing charming objects, and hearing sweet sounds, then in all probability, without being aware of it, he remembers in his mind the friendships of former births firmly rooted in his heart."

रम्याणि वीच्य मधुरांश्च निशम्य शब्दान्

पर्युत्सुकीभवति यत्सुखितोऽपि जन्तुः

तच्चेतसा स्मरति नूनमबोधपूर्वं

भावस्थिराणि जनमान्तरसौहृदानि

Even in Manu's time it was an accepted dogma, that the Souls of men, popularly regarded as emanations from the Deity, might descend into the bodies of animals and trees, or rise to those of higher beings. It was therefore an easy expansion of such a doctrine to imagine the "Divine Soul" itself as passing through various stages of incarnation for the delivery of the World from the effect of evil and sin, and for the maintenance of order in the whole cycle of Creation. ("Indian Wisdom," p. 336.)

Thus began the great series of the Ten Avatára, or the Deity born as an animal, or a man, for the benefit of mankind:

> Three times as animals.
> Once as half man and half animal.
> Five times as man.
> Once still to come, when the World has become wholly depraved, seated on a white horse in the skies, with a drawn sword in his hand.

Manu, the great codifier of existing oral Law, occupying a position analogous to Confucius, Zoroaster, and Moses, writes (XII, iii, 40, 54, 55):

"An act, either mental, verbal, or corporeal (thoughts, words, or deeds), bears good or evil fruit. The various Transmigrations of men through the highest, middle, and lowest stages, are produced by acts." This triple order implies the passage of the Soul through (1) Deities, (2) Men, (3) Animals, or (4) Plants, according to the dominance of one or other of the three Guna: (1) Goodness, (2) Passion, (3) Darkness: and each of these three degrees has three sub-degrees. Those, who have committed great crimes, pass through terrible Hells for a long series of years, and then pass through various bodies. A Brahman-killer's Soul enters the body of a boar, or an ass: the violator of the bed of a Guru migrates a hundred times into the form of grasses, shrubs, plants, etc.

It is clear from this that, as in all Religious Conceptions, the purest and most modern, the Priesthood had their own way, and maintained their authority of Terrorism of the most debased kind over an abject and ignorant community. The Hell-fire Sermon is not a new, or a local, invention.

G. *The Buddhist.*

I quote the words of Gilbert's "Mikado": "Buddhism makes "the punishment or reward fit the crime or merit. A niggard "is reborn either in a state of suffering, or, if into mankind again, "into a state of abject poverty. A liberal man is reborn rich. "A man, who takes away life, is reborn with a short span of life. "One, who abstains from taking life, is reborn with a long span."

Thus the Soul has to bear the consequences of its own acts only. It is tossed hither and thither at the mercy of a force set in *motion by itself alone*, but which can never be guarded against, because its operation depends on past actions wholly beyond control and even unremembered. Even great genius, and congenital excellence, are not natural gifts, τὰ ἔωρα Θέου, but the result of habits formed, and powers developed, through a succession of previous existences. So, again, sufferings of all kind, and moral depravity, are simply the consequence of acts done by each Soul of its own free will in former bodies, which acts exert upon that Soul an irresistible Power, called very significantly Adṛishṭá, because felt and not seen. ("Indian Wisdom," pp. 68, 69.)

When the chief Lama of Tibet dies, it is presumed, that his Soul has passed into some body, and that body must be looked for, and placed on the throne of the deceased. A search is made for a body with certain marks, which are presumed to indicate the presence of the late Lama, and when found he is hailed as successor. The same thing happened, when the Sacred Bull died in Egypt: the Priests had to look out for another Bull, with marks indicating its fitness. The mode of election of the Pope of the Romish Church is something in the same way, but meaner motives there exercise their influence. In the "Cariyá Pítaka" of the Páli Sacred Books the principle is laid down, that the qualifications necessary for making a Buddha cannot be acquired during, and do not depend on the action of, one life only, but are the last result of many deeds *performed through a long series of consecutive lives.*

Although the Idea, that every man had passed through many existences before his birth on earth, and will pass through many more after his death, was distinctly borrowed from Hindu writers, yet the honour of first and solely employing the stories of previous births for educational purposes, and to inculcate great lessons of Morality, must be attributed to Buddha and his followers. This fact was always known to the limited circle of those, who cared for this Branch of Science; but in 1895 the first volume of a work was published by the Cambridge University Press, which introduces the subject to the general public. The volume is entitled "The Játaka, or Stories of the Buddha's Former Births," translated from the Páli by various hands under the Editorship of Professor E. B. Cowell of Cambridge.

Now unquestionably the date of these Stories can be carried back to the date of the Council of Vesáli, 380 B.C.: this is important, as it places them anterior to, and independent of, any Christian influence. The art of Alphabetic writing no doubt existed in India at that period, as testified by the Rock-Inscriptions of Asóka, so that date, if arrived at on literary grounds, can be accepted on Palaeographic grounds; but a material corroboration has also been supplied by the sculptures on the carvings of the railing of the shrines of Sanchi, Amaraváti, and Bharhut, where the titles of the Játaka are clearly inscribed on some of the carvings, and the date of the erection of these shrines has been arrived at on independent grounds. And a remarkable confirmation is found in the Travels of Fah Hian, who, when he visited Ceylon, 400 A.D., saw representations of the 500 bodily forms assumed by Buddha in his successive births, and these legends were habitually made use of to illustrate the teaching of Buddhist Doctrine.

It is quite uncertain, when they were collected into a systematic volume like the present Játaka: no doubt they were first orally delivered from time to time; then gradually they were copied into one volume. Probably the Christian New Testament came together in the same manner. They are all in the Páli Language. The first volume of the Edition contains 150 Birth Stories, partly prose, and partly verse; and each consists of (1) a Preface, which is the story of the Present, detailing how it happened that Buddha was led to tell the story; (2) the story of the birth; (3) a short Summary, in which Buddha identifies the actions, for to Buddha is attributed the power claimed by Pythagoras of remembering on a gigantic scale all the transactions of his previous existence. Every story is illustrated by one or more poetic couplets, or Gatha, uttered by Buddha, to point the moral of the tale. The Language of the Gatha is much more archaic than that of the story, and some might think, that they were the kernel of the story; however, in the opinion of others the Language of the Stories may indeed be later, but they are merely the redaction into writing of materials handed down orally from the earliest period: the Stories were necessarily anterior to the Gatha, though not necessarily in the same words.

Professor Fausböll, of Copenhagen, is the sole Editor of the Páli Text, five volumes of which have appeared. The Translation is conducted by a band of friends, who employ a uniformity of technical terms and transliteration, and certain common principles of Translation.

But it is not the first attempt, for the first volume is dedicated by the author to Professor Rhys Davids, his friend and preceptor, and in the Preface we learn that in 1880 the Professor published one volume containing the "Nidhána-Katha," or complete History of Buddha, both before and during his last birth, and 40 stories: his work ceased there, and it has been since taken up by his friends and pupils. The 40 stories of the earlier volume appear retranslated in the later work as the first 40 of the 150, which it contains.

But the Introduction to Professor Rhys Davids' work above alluded to, entitled " Buddhist Birth Stories," in Trübner's Series, is well worth noticing: it occupies pp. i–lxxxvii of the volume.

He calls attention to the fact, that the fairy-tales, parables, fables, riddles, and comic and moral stories, of the Buddhist Collection bear a striking resemblance to similar ones current in West Asia or Europe. Now, in many instances this resemblance is due to the fact, that they were borrowed from the Buddhist ones. A second fact is, that these stories contain the oldest, most complete, and most important, Collection of Folklore extant. I merely mention these facts, but they have no relation to the subject-matter of this Essay, which is confined to the consideration of the great Problem of the Transmigration of Souls, and the power to recollect the events of previous lives, indicating a continuity of thought from one life to another. The chief Collections of Stories of this kind, which grew out of this fundamental source, are:

Játaka-mala (in Sanskrit),
Pancha-Tantra, alias Hítopadésha (in Sanskrit),
Kálilag and Dámanag (in Syriac),
Kálilut and Dámanat (in Arabic),
"Arabian Nights" (in Arabic),
Aesop's Fables (in Greek),
Phaedrus (in Latin),

and the great crop of modern European Folklore, and Beast-Stories.

Professor Rhys Davids gives us in his Preface the accepted theory as to the mode, in which the Páli Játaka Book came into existence. Their origin is due to "the Religious Faith of the " Early Indian Buddhists, who not only repeated a number of " fables, parables, and stories, ascribed to the Buddha, but gave " them a peculiar sacredness and special Religious signification " by identifying the best character in each with the Buddha " himself in some previous birth." The parables and fables, for they were no more, became their Játaka, a word invented to distinguish the stories thus sanctified. We find the word in the Inscription of the Buddhist Tope at Bharhut, and it clearly must have been a long recognized term to be thus honoured. Gradually came the time for collecting the scattered Játaka into a volume, and this probably took place before the Council of Vesáli, 380 B.C. A tradition as to the time and occasion, at or on which they were uttered, may have given rise to the earliest Introductory Story. They were written in the Páli Language, carried to Ceylon about 200 B.C., and, with the exception of the verses at the close of each, translated into Sinhalese. About the Fifth century A.D. an unknown Author retranslated them into Páli, and compiled the volume now translated into English.

It is a remarkable and incontestable fact, that Buddha taught by *Parables*, but no *Miracles* are imputed to him.

Professor Rhys Davids, at page lxxv of his Preface, and in his "Hibbert Lectures," pp. 88-109, lays stress on the real meaning of Transmigration to the Buddhist. It is not the passage of a Soul from one body to another, for the Buddhists do not admit of the existence of a Soul, or of a God. The Doctrine is somewhat intricate, and is fully explained in the "Manual of Buddhism" by the same author, pp. 99-106; and perhaps what does take place, may better be described as "Transmigration of *Character*," for it is entirely independent of the Idea of the existence within each body of a distinct Soul, Ghost, or Spirit. The Bodhisat is not supposed to have a Soul, which on the death of one body is transferred to another, but to be the inheritor of the *Karma*, or *Character*, acquired by previous Bodhisats.

The insight and goodness, the moral and intellectual perfection, which constitute Buddhahood, could not according to the Buddhist theory be acquired in one lifetime. They were the accumulated result of the continued effort of many generations of successive Bodhisats. The only thing, which continues to exist, when a man dies, is his Karma, the result of his words, thoughts, and deeds, literally his "doing"; and the curious Idea, that the result is concentrated in some new individual, is due to the older Idea of Soul.

Professor Rhys Davids, at p. 114 of his "Hibbert Lectures," 1881, sums up the Philosophy of the Idea as follows:

" Predestination is the logical expression from the Monotheistic
" point of view of the weight of the Universe arrayed against the
" Individual. Pre-existence, or that part of the Transmigration of
" Karma, which is insisted upon in the early Buddhism, is an
" ethical meeting of the same difficulty.

" The fact, underlying all these theories, is acknowledged to be
" a very real one : the history of an individual does not begin with

" his birth. He has been endless generations in making, and he
" cannot sever himself from his surroundings.

* * * * * * *

" A great American writer says, that it was a poetic attempt to
" lift this mountain of Fate, when the Hindu said: 'Fate is nothing,
" but the deeds committed in a previous existence.' Schelling
" writes: 'There is in every man a certain feeling, that he has
" been what he is from all eternity.' We may put a newer and
" deeper meaning into the words of the poet :

" ' Our deeds follow us from afar,
" And what we have been makes us what we are.' "

---

3. The Modern Aspect.

It is no longer a question of Religious Dogma or Philosophy, but a mere sentimental, or intellectual, mystery, yet somehow or other it exists, and there is more in it than appears at first sight. The Poets throw around it a halo of unreality. I have gathered the following thoughts either in print or conversation :

" The Soul sojourning in the earthly body has been likened to
" a current of air drafted through an Aeolian harp, and passing on
" again into the great air of Heaven, but for ever resounding an
" individual chord. So some portion of the Eternal Soul of the
" Universe, dwelling for a while in an earthly body, takes identity,
" and passing onward joins once more, but is not absorbed into the
" Universal Soul, so as to lose absolutely its own identity."

Let me quote Wordsworth's celebrated Ode on the " Intimations of Immortality from Recollections of Early Childhood." The idea of Metempsychósis underlies the whole Poem.

" The sunshine is a glorious birth ;
" But yet I know, where'er I go,
" That there hath past away a glory from the Earth.

* * * * *

" But there's a tree, of many, one,
" A single Field, which I have looked upon,
" Both of them speak of something that is gone :
" The Pansy at my feet
" Doth the same tale repeat :
" Whither is fled the visionary gleam ?
" Where is it now, the glory and the dream ?

" Our birth is but a sleep and a forgetting:
" The Soul, that rises with us, our Life's Star,
    " Hath had elsewhere its setting,
    " And cometh from afar :
    " Not in entire forgetfulness,
    " And not in utter nakedness,
" But trailing clouds of Glory do we come
    " From God, who is our Home :
" Heaven lies about us in our infancy !
" Shades of the prison-house begin to close
    " Upon the growing Boy,
" But He beholds the Light, and whence it flows,
    " He sees it in his joy.

   * * * * *

" Earth fills her lap with pleasures of her own.

   * * * * *

    " And no unworthy aim,
    " The homely Nurse doth all she can
" To make her Foster-child, her Inmate Man,
    " Forget the Glories he hath known,
" And that Imperial Palace whence he came.

   * * * * *

    " But for those first affections,
    " Those shadowy recollections,
    " Which, be they what they may,
" Are yet the fountain-light of all our day . . . .

   * * * * *

" Our Souls have sight of that Immortal Sea,
    " Which brought us hither,
    " Can in a moment travel thither."

I follow with a quotation from Tennyson's " Two Voices " :

    " It may be that no life is found,
    " Which only to one engine bound
    " Falls off, but cycles always round.

    " As old mythologies relate,
    " Some draught of Lethe might await
    " The slipping through from state to state.

    " As here we find in trances men
    " Forget the dream, that happens then,
    " Until they fall in trance again,

"So might we, if our state were such,
"As one before, remember much,
"For those two likes might meet and touch.

"But, if I lapsed from nobler place,
"Some legend of a fallen race
"Alone might hint of my disgrace;

"Some vague emotion of delight
"In gazing up an Alpine height,
"Some yearning toward the lamps of night.

"Or, if through lower lives I came,
"Tho' all experience past became
"Consolidate in mind and frame,

"I might forget my weaker lot,
"For is not our first year forgot?
"The haunts of memory echo not.

"Much more, if first I floated free,
"As naked essence must I be
"Incompetent of memory:

"For memory dealing but with time,
"And he with matter, could she climb
"Beyond her own material prime?

"Moreover, something is or seems,
"That touches me with mystic gleams
"Like glimpses of forgotten dreams:

"Of something felt like something here,
"Of something done, I know not where,
"Such as no language may declare."

This will find an echo in the Souls of many. Do we not seem, in our musing hours, to have heard something long before, to have thought some thought, to have uttered some word, to have seen some landscape, in a previous existence, or under different circumstances? This happens to fresh young minds oftener than to the jaded intellects of those in middle life or old age. Have we not sometimes felt, that we have fallen from a higher intellectual and spiritual age somewhere, that we understood things better once, which seem now a puzzle? Of course, Dreams develop these feelings, specially Day-Dreams, where the direction of the thoughts are guided by the will, which is not in the torpor of sleep: and sweet Music helps it.

In Charles Dickens's "Dombey and Son," p. 210 of the original Edition, we come unexpectedly on the following words: "an undeveloped recollection of a previous state of existence."

There is a ring of pathos in the lines by that charming writer George Eliot:

"Oh may I join the choir invisible
"Of those immortal dead, *who live again*
"*In minds made better by their presence*: live
"In pulses stirred to generosity,
"In deeds of daring rectitude, in scorn
"For miserable aims that end in self,
"In thoughts sublime that pierce the night-like stars,
"And with their mild persistence urge men's search
"To vaster issues   .   .   .   .
"This is life to come."

Professor Rhys Davids admits, that there is some analogy between this beautiful sentiment of the modern Positivist and the Buddhist doctrine of Karma; but the modern Poet is thinking of the Future, the ancient Prophet dwells on the Past.

In Archbishop Trench's "Day of Death" occur the following lines:

"Or the Soul long strives in vain
"To escape with toil and pain,
"From its half-divided chain":

which I fifty-five years ago, at Naples, rendered into monkish Latin:

"An se demum curâ plena
"Expedibit multâ poenâ
"Semiruptâ Mens catenâ?"

We recollect the Emperor Hadrian's address to his Soul:

"Animula vagula blandula,
"Hospes comesque corporis,
"Quos nunc abibis in locos?
"Pallidula rigida nudula,
"Nec, ut ante, dabis jocos":

rendered so nobly by the Poet Pope:

"Poor little pretty fluttering thing,
"Must we no longer live together?
"And dost thou prune thy timid wing,
"And take thy flight, thou knowest not whither?"

I finally quote one living Poet, Mr. Lecky:

> " So in our dreams some glimpse appears,
> " Though soon it fades again,
> " How other lands, or times, or spheres,
> " Might make us other men.
>
> " Now half our being lies in trance,
> " Nor joy, nor sorrow, brings,
> " Unless the hand of circumstance
> " Can touch the latent strings.
>
> " We know not fully what we are,
> " Still less what we might be,
> " But hear *faint voices from the far,*
> " *Dim lands beyond the sea!*"

Some thoughts rise in my mind. Can it be, that such a Divine Creation as a Soul can only be used for one brief life, perhaps a very brief one indeed of a few summers, perhaps the tenant of a Human form unworthy of it, owing to want of Culture, or absence of Virtue?

> " Perhaps in this neglected spot is laid
> " Some Soul once pregnant with celestial fire :
> " Hands that the rod of Empire might have swayed,
> " Or waked to ecstasy the living lyre."
>
> GRAY's *Elegy.*

Would not a Soul be strengthened for the daily combat of life by undergoing different conditions of its poor mortal place of temporary habitation, different environments of the mortal coil, different experiences of Human vicissitudes? On the other hand, would not a Soul, having left a pure and holy tenement, be defiled and degraded by contact with some base Human embodiment of Carnality, Vice, and Degradation, which the Holy Spirit, which deigns to dwell with Man, has abandoned in despair and anger?

What becomes of the accumulated Millions of Souls, if after the accomplishment of one brief term of service, they are never employed again? Do they fade like the leaves of the forest in Autumn, having done what they were created to do? What is the meaning of absorption into the Divine Essence, or, as the Christian Minister fondly puts it, "being with Christ"? The whole subject is a mystery.

What is the Soul (Ψυχή, Psyché)? Can it die? Some say that it can, and quote the New Testament: "Fear Him, who is able to destroy both Soul (Ψυχή) and Body (Σώμα) in Gehenna."

It is vain to argue on such a subject: the intellect is finite, and the subject of this question is infinite.

But there is a third indwelling part of the "*Homo*," which appears before us: the Spirit (Πνεῦμα). This comes of God, and is God, and can certainly never die, and can certainly leave the body; but this lies outside the subject of this Essay, which is restricted to the opinions formed by men at different periods, and in different countries, and degrees of Culture, as to the Transmigration of the Soul (Ψυχη) from one Body (Σώμα) to another.

Sometimes we come into contact with a young creature, whose Soul seems fresh from Heaven, and fit for Heaven. Having been blessed with the tenement of a docile body, the two entities, Soul and Body, move in unison: they ripen fast, and are soon removed. Sometimes we meet, or hear of, persons, who seem devoid of Soul altogether. Again, we come upon persons, who seem to have inherited an evil Soul: some are fierce and bitter in temperament, who, if they have not inherited these characteristics, are qualifying at the next birth to enter a tiger; some are gross and carnal, who are qualifying to pass into swine at the next opportunity.

Again, there are instances of mysterious attraction betwixt Soul and Soul (I do not allude to the attractions of carnal Earthly Love): there exists sometimes a wonderful feeling, that creates a link between two Souls, though they occupied their brief earthly span two or three centuries apart; yet there seems to be a mysterious union, the "*idem sentire de rebus Humanis et Divinis.*" Has not some one unexpectedly come upon passages in some book, which existed before his birth, but never heard of till lately, which reveal to him his own hidden thoughts, passing under review the mysterious Problem of Self, the World, and God, suggesting solutions, long before revealed to him in his musings by day, or his waking hours by night? Still more wonderful is the solution of hard problems, which he has striven for in vain, sought for from his contemporaries without success, but revealed to his astonished eyes in a book of the last century. There must surely be some affinity of that portion of us, which is Divine, with that which existed, or exists in others. I do not ask for sensational common-form expressions of the ignorant formularist, whether Hindu, Buddhist, Mahometan, or Christian, who has not even thought out the problem, but the reverential humble expressions of thought of one, who

"extra
"Processit longè flammantia moenia mundi,
"Atque omne immensum peragravit mente animoque."
LUCRETIUS.

Then clearly there are sins peculiar to the body, in which the enlightened Soul can take no pleasure, carnal appetites, low and evil desires, envy, hatred, and malice. A man's "better self" loathes such things, but has to endure them in an ill-assorted union. The great Soul will not condescend to profit by the loss of his neighbour, will not sell its purity for gold, will not utter a lie even for its own advantage, is ready to sacrifice itself for the benefit of others, looks on the world around with a pitying eye, but willing to continue in its mortal tenement, if it can benefit the poor and suffering. "Altruism," not "Egoism," is the Law of its Nature, following the example of Gautama Buddha, who was the first to propound the noble Idea of "Loving others better than one's self," and the precepts given Five centuries later by One Greater than the Buddha. On the other hand, in a comparatively innocuous, quiescent, body, there are grievous sins of the Soul, of which the Body has no cognizance, such as Denial of the Lord, who bought us, Worldliness, Lust for Power, such as Satan offered to the Lord at the Temptation, Lust for Wealth, such as that of the Rich Man in the Parable, whose Soul in the midst of his enjoyments that very night was required.

It is necessary to draw one line absolutely: a Soul is a Soul, a body is a body; the Soul is an eternal entity, the body is a perishable atom: and in that last particular all creatures having life are on the same level. When the breath of life departs, the poor clay-tenement returns to dust. But the incidence of death was not written for the Soul. Now we know, as a positive fact, that there is an ineffaceable division between the "genus *Homo*," and the rest of the Animal-Creation. The Sacred Books of every Religion may not affirm it, but it is a fact, which is written in clear letters in the History of the World, that the intelligence of animals, such as the Elephant, the Horse, the Dog, and the Cat, though most worthy of note, is limited, and no degree of Culture would carry it beyond certain limited boundaries, or prolong it from generation to generation; while the intelligence of the "genus *Homo*" is unlimited: even now it is only in the course of development. Things are known to us at the close of the Nineteenth century absolutely unknown, and undreamed of, at the close of the Eighteenth century. To the "genus *Homo*" alone has been conceded the two great congenital gifts of (1) Articulate Speech, (2) a Religious Instinct. Therefore Transmigration of a Soul into the body of an animal, not calculated to be the tenement of a Soul, is a thing impossible.

The gist of the matter is, that in all speculations of men of the Nineteenth century, and in all reverential communings with the Soul as to its future destiny after its parting from the mortal tenement, in which it is now included, there are but two alternatives:

A. "To be with Christ" in a mysterious, indefinable, state of existence, and yet non-existence: this is the fond vision of holy men. The reply to the inquirer is an illustration of "*Obscurum per obscurius.*"

No one ever came back, and revealed the mystery beyond the tomb. The Old and New Testaments are silent. The sad lines of the late Poet Laureate come back to us:

" When Lazarus left his charnel-cave,
   " And home to Mary's house return'd,
   " Was this demanded, if he yearn'd
" To hear her weeping by his grave?

" ' Where wert thou, brother, those four days?'
   " There lives no record of reply,
   " Which telling what it is to die
" Had surely added praise to praise.

" Behold a man raised up by Christ!
   " The rest remaineth unreveal'd:
   " He told it not; or something seal'd
" The lips of that Evangelist."

TENNYSON: *In Memoriam,* xxxi.

B. To transmigrate into another individual body of the "genus *Homo.*"

The theory of Purgatory is not only unscriptural, but a mere intellectual delusion. If sins are to be purged after death, it seems more reasonable, that they should be purged under the same conditions as those, in which they were committed in this mortal life: in practice it appears to be only a machinery for bringing money to the Priesthood.

My thoughts pass from the dying ejaculations of the great Roman Emperor, quoted above, who was denied the opportunity of knowing Christ, to the Soul of the young man of our own time, who had been chosen from his boyhood, had been consecrated in the bloom of his youth, to the service of his Master; to whom the gift had been conceded of an ingenuous countenance, on which the word 'Aγάπη, not Ἔρως, was written, from whose lips flowed words that burn, the reflection of thought, that breathed; whose life represented the simplicity, the holiness, the self-sacrifice, the high desire, the very Christ, whom he preached; whose Soul, having found a mortal tenement worthy of the habitation of its Divine Essence, rejoiced in the discharge of holy duties, the daily something accomplished, something done. Many the poor sinning brother and sister were by him brought to Christ on the dying bed in the Hospital; the happy Soul of the Teacher lending itself in deep sympathy, and pure aim, to the poor distracted, trembling, hopeless, Soul of the unhappy sinner. No pride there: but for God's Grace the Soul of the saved one would have been in the same plight as the Soul of the all but lost one; for with God there is no προσωπολήψις, and the poor Human race are all on the same level, the certainty of condemnation but for the Saviour.

Him, the tenement of such a Soul, a fever acquired in his holy visiting of the sick, laid low, and the term of his days was accomplished; there was no murmur on his part. He had done what he could, and filled up the little space, for which he was ordained to glorify God; the ministration of his Master only lasted three years, was not that sufficient for him also? The example of his death is even more precious than his life: he has his reward. Better to die thus.

"ὃν ὁ Θεὸς φιλεῖ θνήσκει νέος."

But for the poor Soul, for it there is no death: of it may be said:

"It hoped that with the brave and strong
"Its destined course might lie,
"To toil amidst the busy throng,
"With purpose pure and high."

ANN BRONTE.

"Hei mihi! quid feci? unde lapsus sum?"

It does not die like the poor clay-tenement; it is still for ever with the Lord: in its deep humility it pleads nothing in its own favour, for it had only done its duty and is content. But still it pants for new opportunities to save Souls: it pines for re-embodiment in another weak vessel: it thinks of the hospital fever-struck patient with no fellow-Christian near to whisper words of Repentance, Pardon, and Peace: it is ready: can we believe, that Aeons of unemployed happiness will satisfy the inexhaustible desire of the Ψυχή and Πνεῦμα to do their Master's work. Can Idleness be bliss to a Soul, which during its short period of embodiment was in ceaseless holy activity, doing the Lord's work among his fellow-creatures?

Another point of view is the comforting one, that being allowed to tread the Earth again, a great unrepenting sinner has a chance of escaping the awful penalties, whatever may be the correct rendering of the word αἰώνιον, "for a season," as in Philemon, 15, or "everlasting," "age-lasting," as in Matthew, xviii, 8. The idea, that a life of a few summers, or of a few days, decides the fate of a poor

Soul for Eternity, is too awful to be entertained. To what an extent the preponderant weight of a mere dogma of a man in the Middle Ages can influence good holy weak men, is evidenced by the two following stanzas in the " Day of Doom," by Michael Wigglesworth, which is still read in Christian New England. "Reprobate" (in the technical sense) Infants are in his poem summoned to judgment.

> " Then to the Bar they all drew near,
> " Who died in infancy,
> " And never had, or good or bad,
> " Effected personally."

The little children cry out, pleading their innocence, but are rebuked as sinners; every sin is a crime.

> " A crime it is: therefore in bliss,
> " You may not hope to dwell:
> " But unto you I shall allow
> " The easiest room in Hell."

Cases are frequent of men repenting in middle life, or in advanced years, and passing from Death unto Life, because the chance was given them. There is no limit to the Mercies of God; but Justice must be combined with Love. In India fifty years ago, two very young officers were driving home from the Regimental mess in a state of intoxication; they had not counted twenty summers, and were still in the blind folly of youth, and had commenced a life of profligacy. Their vehicle was upset, and one was cast out dead; the other was taken to the hospital with a compound fracture of both legs: there he lingered under the blessed influences of a Sister of the Hospital, an angel in the form of a woman, and eventually came out a changed man, lived a long life of holy benevolence, and then entered into his rest. Let us think of the poor lad, the thread of whose life was snapped in the midst of his sins. "Nobody ever spoke to me," a poor dying lad once said to a kindly visitor in India, who came to soothe his last repentant hours. He had had previously no chance given him, no opportunity of recovering his self-control. Setting aside as impossible the idea of Everlasting Torture in such, or in any, case, perhaps in a new environment a better life might be spent: and the Soul of the poor lad, whose body perished while still in his teens, in a new incarnation might have been blessed with a fresh Revelation of Christ, and, if needs be, suffer, but be patient and strong, and try to atone for past errors.

As long as the heart beats with Human affections, as long as the Soul gives birth to Divine aspirations, this wondrous speculation will be entertained.

" Πῶς γενόμην; πόθεν εἰμί; τίνος χάριν ἦλθον; ἀπελθεῖν;
" Πῶς δύναμαι τι μαθεῖν, μηδὲν ἐπιστάμενος;
" Οὐδὲν ἐὼν γενόμην· πάλιν ἔσσομαι, ὡς πάρος ἦα,
" Οὐδέν, καὶ μηδέν, τῶν μερόπων τὸ γένος."
Anthologia Palatina, viii, 118.

The poor vile body is indeed mortal; but the Soul is Immortal. Shall we not say with Walter Pater ("Plato and Platonism," p. 64): "The teaching of Pythagoras, like all the graver utterances
" of primitive Greek Philosophy, *is an instinct of the Human mind*
" *itself*, and therefore a constant Tradition in Human History,
" *which will ever recur*, fortifying this or that Soul, here or there,
" in a part at least of that old sanguine assurance about itself"?

To many, much that has been written in this my last Chapter may appear as a dream, and it may please those, who are narrow-minded, and incapable of reflection on the History of the Past, and unsusceptible of Reverential Thought as to the Future, to describe Chapters I and II as "the teaching of Satan," which is the general description in certain Religious and Missionary circles of the Religious Convictions of the Elder World. Be it so!
"*Sursum corda.*"

November, 1897.

BIBLIOGRAPHY.

	PAGE
Heráclitus Pónticus	110
Horatius Flaccus : Odes, I	110
Plato : Dialogues	110–114
Milton : "Comus"	112
Strabo, IV	114
Valerius Maximus, V	114
Diodorus, VI	114
Dr. F. B. Jevons : "History of Religion"	114
Authoress of "Sculptured Tombs of Hellas" : *Edinburgh Review*, April, 1897	115
Shakespeare : "Measure for Measure"	116
Virgil : "Aeneid," VI	116
Homer : "Odyssey," XI	117
(Worsley's Translation of above.)	117
Virgil : "Aeneid," VI	117
Virgil : "Aeneid," III	118
Ovid : "Metamorphoses"	118
Lucan : "Pharsalia"	118
Julius Caesar : "De Bello Gallico"	119
Claudian	119
Irish Legend : "Book of Balimote"	119
Herodotus, II	120
Frazer : "Golden Bough"	121
Tylor : "Primitive Man"	121
Henry Stanley : "In Darkest Africa"	121
The New Testament	121
Bishop Lightfoot of Durham	122
Shechter : "Studies in Judaism"	122
Ezekiel, xviii	123
The New Testament	123
Gratz : "Zohar"	124
Josephus : "Antiquities of the Jews," "Wars of the Jews" ...	124
Dr. Ginsburg : Smith's "Dictionary of Christian Biography"	124
New Testament : Romans, ix, 11	124
"Acta Martyrum." 1748 A.D.	125
Neander : Church History, II, 218	125
Baidawi : Commentary on "Súra," III, 165	125
Omar Khaiyyam	125

	PAGE
Professor E. G. Browne, Pembroke College, Cambridge: "New History of the Báb," pp. 334-8	125
Másnavi	126
Professor Browne : "Year amongst the Persians"	126
Satapátha-Bráhmana ("Indian Wisdom," p. 34)	127
Professor Rhys Davids : "Hibbert Lectures"	127, 135
Kaushítaki Bráhmana Upanishad	127
Vishnu Purána, translated by R. N. Cust	128
Kalidása : "Sakóntala"	131
Manu ("Indian Wisdom," p. 336)	131
Manu, XII, iii, 40, 54, 55	131
Gilbert : "Mikado"	132
Monier-Williams : "Indian Wisdom," pp. 68-9	132
"Cariyá Pítaka" (Pali)	132
Professor E. B. Cowell, Cambridge : "The Játaka of Buddha" (translation)	133
Professor Fausböll, Copenhagen : "The Játaka of Buddha" (text)	134
Professor Rhys Davids : Preface to "Nidhána-Katha"	134
Professor Rhys Davids : "Manual of Buddhism" (S.P.C.K.)	135
Wordsworth : Ode on the "Intimations of Immortality from Recollections of Early Childhood"	136
Tennyson : "Two Voices"	137
Charles Dickens : "Dombey and Son," p. 210 of Original Edition	139
Archbishop Trench : "Day of Death"	139
(R. N. Cust : Latin translation of the above.)	139
"Farewell of Emperor Hadrian to his Soul"	139
(Translation of above by Pope.)	139
Poem by Mr. Lecky	140
Gray : "Elegy in a Country Churchyard"	140
New Testament : Matthew, x, 28	140
Lucretius	141
Tennyson : "In Memoriam," xxxi	143
Ann Bronte	144
Michael Wigglesworth : "Day of Doom"	145
"Anthologia Palatina," viii, 118	146
Walter Pater : "Plato and Platonism," p. 64	146

BOOKS READ, BUT NOT QUOTED.

F. Peek : "Aeonian Metempsychósis" (*Contemporary Review*).
"Encyclopaedia Britannica," 9th Edition.
Monier-Williams : "Religious Thought in India."

www.ingramcontent.com/pod-product-compliance
Lightning Source LLC
Chambersburg PA
CBHW030349170426
43202CB00010B/1312